C000264460

City of Manchester

Manchester

in the Great War

Your Towns and Cities in the Great War

City of Manchester

in the Great War

Glynis Greenman

Pen & Sword
MILITARY

First published in Great Britain in 2017 by
PEN & SWORD MILITARY
An imprint of
Pen & Sword Books Ltd
47 Church Street
Barnsley
South Yorkshire
S70 2AS

Copyright © Glynis Greenman, 2017

ISBN 978-1-47383-775-1

The right of Glynis Greenman to be identified as the author of this work
has been asserted by her in accordance with the Copyright, Designs and
Patents Act 1988.

A CIP catalogue record for this book is available from the British Library.

All rights reserved. No part of this book may be reproduced or transmitted
in any form or by any means, electronic or mechanical including
photocopying, recording or by any information storage and retrieval
system, without permission from the Publisher in writing.

Typeset by Concept, Huddersfield, West Yorkshire HD4 5JL.
Printed and bound in England by CPI Group (UK) Ltd,
Croydon CR0 4YY.

Pen & Sword Books Ltd incorporates the imprints of Pen & Sword
Archaeology, Atlas, Aviation, Battleground, Discovery, Family History,
History, Maritime, Military, Naval, Politics, Railways, Select,
Social History, Transport, True Crime, and Claymore Press,
Frontline Books, Leo Cooper, Praetorian Press, Remember When,
Seaforth Publishing and Wharncliffe.

For a complete list of Pen & Sword titles please contact
PEN & SWORD BOOKS LIMITED
47 Church Street, Barnsley, South Yorkshire, S70 2AS, England
E-mail: enquiries@pen-and-sword.co.uk
Website: www.pen-and-sword.co.uk

Contents

Dedication

To all those who worked, suffered and died in the inner-city mill-scapes of Manchester that made Britain great and yet who somehow found the additional reserves of strength, adaptability and determination to help defeat the Kaiser – and especially to all those Mancunians who 'gave their today for our tomorrow' in the Great War.

Acknowledgments

Grateful thanks are due to the *Manchester Guardian* for the use of their newspaper archives; to Manchester Central Library for all their assistance and the excellent illustrations from their Local Studies Collection; to the editorial team at Pen & Sword and to Roni Wilkinson, Commissioning Editor for Pen & Sword; to family and friends for their patience and understanding; and to all those Mancunians who did their city proud in times of need.

Introduction

⌐~⭤⭤⭤⭤~⌐

Manchester is a large and ever-expanding city, the 'second city' of England, the proposed 'powerhouse of the North'. Today the city centre is a relatively small area surrounded by thirty suburbs which in turn are surrounded by nine or ten large towns and Metropolitan Council areas. The current city centre is the very heart of the city around Piccadilly, Market Street, Long Millgate, St Ann's Square, Deansgate, Albert Square, St Peter's Square and Castlefield. During the Great War, however, delineations were less clear and the city centre tended to include the inner-city suburbs of Ancoats, Chorlton-on-Medlock, Hulme, and the western parts of Ardwick, Rusholme and Openshaw. All these places were originally villages which became subsumed as 'Cottonopolis' and the Industrial Revolution spread, although they are now emerging as separate entities once more with their own individual characters. For the purposes of this book, however, some of the inner suburbs will form a part of the story.

The history of Manchester stretches back to the New Stone Age when farming settlements first began to emerge. The town had long been recognized as an important trading and textile centre in Roman, Viking and Medieval times, but its real moment of fame came with the introduction of the cotton mills during the late 1770s. Successful cotton manufacture requires certain climatic conditions and soft water. Manchester fitted the bill and the town never looked back, finally achieving city status in 1853. The new city was rich and prosperous for a comparative few, but many of its working-class inhabitants were forced to live in unbelievable poverty and squalor 'in sties of filth and darkness'. Life expectancy was low and infant mortality was high. Cholera was rife and Friedrich Engels called Manchester 'Hell upon Earth', especially the Angel Meadow area on the northern edge of the city centre. It really was a 'tale of two cities', a situation recognized by a number of the privileged minority, some of whom did their best to improve conditions. Although not realized at the time,

St Ann's Church, St Ann's Square Manchester. (*Courtesy of Manchester Central Library Local Studies Collection*)

the beginning of the end for 'Cottonopolis' was the American Civil War (1861–5) when the supply of American cotton dried up and the mills practically ceased production. However, despite everything, the citizens of Manchester supported Abraham Lincoln and those opposing slavery and there is a commemorative statue of him in Lincoln Square near the Town Hall.

By the time of the Great War the cotton industry was facing severe difficulties although the immediate impact of the outbreak of the Great War was a swansong and 1914 proved to be the most prosperous year the industry had ever known. It was not to last and many inhabitants of Manchester would be left in dirty, polluted, poverty-stricken surroundings to support both themselves and an expensive war abroad as best they could while facing, for the first time, the terrors of aerial bombardment, as well as the added deprivations to their already poor standard of living and the unprecedented loss of a whole generation of young men. It is a great testament to their courage, grit and stoicism that Manchester folk determined, despite all their problems and hardships, to do everything they possibly could to support the Home Front and the troops abroad so that the Kaiser would not win the war.

CHAPTER 1

1914

The Great War began for Manchester, and the *Manchester Guardian* in particular, long before the first shot was fired. Manchester had been aware of the growing crisis in Europe for some time over the threat of war amid fears over rising prices and threats to British concerns abroad, especially trade. The Lord Mayor was particularly concerned about food sources, food supplies and increasing food prices. Initial worries seemed to be over trade and profits rather than people but the two were interlinked. The Manchester branch of the Norman Ansell League, whose function was to 'pursue, in times of war or peace, an international education crusade against ignorant mob jingoism aiming at a world-wide education of public opinion on the complete futility of war', believed that if only this process had begun sooner the present situation would not have arisen. The *Jewish Chronicle* did not see why 'Great Britain should send the flower of its manhood to defend Russian interests'. A resolution was passed by the British section of the International Socialist Bureau, which was endorsed by the Labour Party, stating 'we view with serious alarm the prospects of a European war into which every European power will be dragged owing to secret alliances and understandings which in their origins were never sanctioned by the nations nor are even now communicated to them'. Charles P. Scott, the editor of the *Manchester Guardian*, fought a personal campaign from its offices in Cross Street, denouncing the war in editorials and declaring it was 'a conspiracy to drag us into a war against England's interests ... it would throw away the progress of half a century ... ', referring no doubt to the Crimean War which had ended in 1856 and the American Civil War which had ended in 1865. He went on to say: 'If we, who might remain neutral, rush into war or let our attitude remain doubtful, it will be both a crime and an act of supreme and gratuitous folly'. He was not alone in his wish for continuing peace. Scott lobbied the Prime Minister, Herbert Asquith, and members of

C.P. Scott, editor of the *Manchester Guardian* in the First World War. (*Courtesy of Manchester Central Library Local Studies Collection*)

the Liberal Party Cabinet and he was supported for a while by *The Times* which believed that the English press should remain neutral. David Lloyd George, then Chancellor of the Exchequer, had been in favour of retaining neutrality and peace, telling Scott on the day war broke out '... that there had been, a clear majority for the "peace party" in the Cabinet only days before' and that only two members of the Cabinet had supported intervention in the war. In fact, Lloyd George came close to resigning in protest over the threat of war. On the last day of July, Scott, learning that British Territorial Reserves had been mobilized and, incandescent with rage at the government's refusal to publicly discuss the possibility of war, wrote a scathing leader for the *Manchester Guardian* 'pinning the blame firmly on a secretive, powerful and irresponsible group of politicians and officials who were not even willing to debate the reasons to go to war in public'. He added 'At the head of affairs is a government which may be bluffing and is fallible ... behind it are strong influences, social and bureaucratic, which are anxious for war ... the House of Commons, which should be the guardian of national interest at such a time as this, is discussing the milk and dairies bill ... but Mr Asquith calls that presenting a united front to the nations of Europe.'

Three days before war was declared Scott pointed out that the treaties signed by Britain, France and Germany in 1870, guaranteeing Belgian neutrality, had expired in 1871. The Germans had already dismissed that treaty as 'just a piece of paper'. In a final plea Scott wrote in his leader on Monday, 3 August, 'this country should not make itself an accessory to the crime against reason and human happiness ... to starve every hope except those that can be indulged by the suffering and impoverishment of others'.

There were many protests about the imminent possibility of war and strongly conflicting views on involvement in such a struggle, as well as pleas for British neutrality (a move backed by the University of Cambridge) but the sticking points were Belgian neutrality, which the Germans seemed intent on violating, and the defence of the English Channel and North Sea if the German fleet chose to use those waters for hostile action against France. The violation of Belgium was said to be a step too far, but it seems it was the threat to the English Channel that finally determined Britain to enter the war. All British naval reserves and volunteers under the age of 55 were called up because of the mood of uncertainty. Most folk had confidence in Sir Edward Grey, the Foreign Secretary, but he could see what was coming and he knew he was powerless to stop it. On the evening of 3 August he remarked gloomily to a friend that 'The lamps are going out all over Europe, we shall not see them lit again in our lifetime'. Crowds gathered outside the offices of the *Manchester Guardian* in

Market Street, waiting and hoping for good news. It did not come and on the following day, 4 August 1914, war was declared. Sir Edward Grey's worst fears had been realized. On that same date a hundred years later lights would be dimmed in private homes and public places all over Britain and at a national memorial service in Westminster Abbey in stark tribute to Sir Edward Grey's words and the subsequent commencement of the Great War.

Crowds waited outside the offices of the *Manchester Guardian* on 4 August, anxious about what might happen. The Boer War, also opposed by the *Guardian*, had only ended twelve years before and few wanted war to happen again and especially so soon. However, after the official declaration of war on the afternoon of the 4th, first reactions to the new war in central Manchester was much the same as in other places. There was an initial enthusiasm to teach the Germans a short, sharp lesson and large numbers of men volunteered immediately for Army service. Within a couple of weeks stories of German atrocities inflicted on Belgium had filtered through amid allegations of unprovoked attacks, brutality, mutilation, rape and 'little children outraged'. Now that war had been officially declared Scott, who used the *Manchester Guardian* and its associated papers to support the decision and the war effort, declaring in his editorial the day after the war had begun that ' ... we ourselves have contended for the neutrality of England to the utmost of our power and with a deep conviction that we were doing our patriotic duty ... some time the responsibility for one of the greatest errors of our history will have to be fixed, but that time is not now ... there is nothing for Englishmen to do now but to stand together and help by every means in their power to the attainment of our common object ... an early and decisive victory over Germany ...'. A prophetic understatement in hindsight.

By the end of August £1,631,000 (£169,757,701 today) had been raised all over the country for the National Relief Fund and it was increasing daily. No casualty lists for the British Expeditionary Force (BEF), sent to support Belgium and France in their fight with Germany, had been received by late August but there was little sign of undue concern over military resources and compulsory conscription was not even considered at this stage at all. However, hardships were already beginning to bite on the Home Front. A patriotic poem had been published in the local newspaper. It was, wrote one Manchester lady, 'the usual thing ... a touching picture of the soldier's wife sitting at home, with her hands in lap, rapt in silent grief and listening breath-lessly for the boom of Belgian bombs'. The reality, as she readily admitted, was somewhat different. Her charlady's husband was a reservist who had re-joined the Colours on the outbreak of war and the said charlady 'is not exactly in a position to make a luxury of grief ... with her husband gone to the front and the Government's sepa-ration allowance slow in coming and amounting to little more than her rent when it comes ...'. The charlady's response to her mistress's enquiries about her husband was pragmatic. 'Can't say how he is not having had a word from him since he went. No, I ain't what you call exactly worrying. Two weeks with nothing coming in and the pawn-shops closed, then eleven bob a week from the Government for self and two kids with seven bob to pay out of that for rent, don't leave much time over for ruminating.' This exchange highlighted the problems faced by many families both in Manchester and all over the country. The loss of the breadwinner, or main wage-earner, left little or no income for their families. Using pawnbrokers was a fact of life for many families so that they could put food on the table each day of the week. Although women worked, they were paid far less than men. A separation allowance was paid to dependants for each family man who enlisted but it was less than adequate. The situation wasn't helped by the fact that, despite these problems, large numbers of landlords saw no reason to suspend their annual rent increases. This forced poorer families, who could no longer afford their rent on a reduced income, to double up with family or friends which led to even more cramped living conditions while a number of properties were left empty. Breaking up a home, however poor, was always heart-breaking, and the storage of furniture or possessions caused financial problems which the government were slow to address.

The charlady also had decided views about the sheer waste of life in any conflict. She told her mistress that if English, French, German and Belgian women were giving their sons to fight out of patriotic love for their countries, then it seemed 'a waste of that love in killing them off in hundreds ...'. Immediately, however, she had the rising costs of living and the welfare of two children to worry about. The *Manchester Guardian* ran detailed economic reports and trade was a key question. Grain, flour and bread prices had already risen, with the price of bacon and other foodstuffs set to rise imminently. The rent took almost two-thirds of her separation allowance. Apart from rent and food there was the cost of fuel and clothing to worry about.

There was no welfare state and if allowances were late families could find themselves going hungry. Hints on economy and cookery were already being published in the papers. Suggestions were made for using more jam and no butter on bread, halving the amount of rice used in rice pudding, making scones from fried porridge, and, most unappetizing of all, to cut the use of vegetables by replacing a second or third vegetable with a purée of potato peelings, stale bread and old vegetable leaves boiled together and mashed through a sieve. There was also encouragement to grow your own but, although this was fine for more rural areas, in the streets of closely packed 'back-to-back' housing in central Manchester that just wasn't an option. Gardens were luxuries reserved for those who could afford better and even a small shared yard at the rear of properties was a luxury in many of the mean streets around the city centre.

'Back-to-backs' had been a means of cramming large numbers of workers into small areas. Two rows of terraced houses would share a single back wall so that there was no back entrance and no back yard. The front doors of these houses opened directly onto the pavement

Bostock's Boots, Market Street, Manchester. (*Courtesy of Manchester Central Library Local Studies Collection*)

and opposite, on each street, would be more rows of 'back-to-backs'. Sharing three of their four walls with other buildings also meant that 'back-to-backs' were dark and poorly ventilated. Only a very few of these 'back-to-back' houses remain today as they contravene a number of public health regulations and they are also considered a fire risk. Some of the smaller houses would be 'one up, one down', consisting of a simple living room cum kitchen with a single sleeping room above. In basement accommodation whole families would have to live, sleep and eat in one room. Most folk aspired to a 'two up, two down' where there was a small front parlour and a larger rear kitchen cum living room with two bedrooms above. Sanitary arrangements involved daily washing in cold water at the kitchen sink, sometimes a tin bath in the kitchen for a quick shallow soak on Friday nights, and communal outdoor toilets. A century on it is fashionable to live in city centres. In 1914 it was fashionable and far healthier in the north-west to live well away from city centres, especially in Manchester, in the outer suburbs of Didsbury, Chorlton-cum-Hardy and Northenden to the south or Blackley and Moston to the north. Some of the worst areas in the inner city were by the River Irk in Angel Meadow, close to Victoria railway station, and also around Ancoats and Little Ireland bordering the Medlock on Oxford Road in Chorlton-on-Medlock and the boundaries of Hulme. Manchester City Council had been making tremendous efforts at slum clearance and replacement by municipal housing, notably the Victoria Square (Ancoats) labourers' dwellings completed in 1894, but, like everywhere else, the Great War brought a full stop to improvements in housing and sanitation. In addition there were major health issues. Cholera, typhoid and TB were rife owing to contaminated water, a lack of hygiene and the cramped squalor in which thousands were forced to live. Epidemics of measles, mumps and influenza would spread rapidly. An equally vicious problem was that of drink. Alcohol provided the only means of escape from the nightmare of 'Cottonopolis' and many spent much of their scant wages on it. Children were expected to work in order to feed themselves and often their parents as well. Their growth was often stunted as a result of poor nutrition. Scurvy (caused by Vitamin C deficiency) and rickets (caused by Vitamin D deficiency) were common.

The young men of central Manchester, however, were quick to volunteer for the Army. Apart from patriotic zeal and duty, for many

Army recruits in Manchester 1914. (*Courtesy of Manchester Central Library Local Studies Collection*)

it was an escape, or so they believed. The Manchester Regiment was an infantry regiment whose headquarters were at Ladysmith Barracks in Ashton-under-Lyne, some seven or eight miles from the City. By 1914 it had two battalions and a number of volunteer battalions which had been known as the Territorials since 1908. The 2nd Manchester Battalion, which had served in the Boer War, left for France in the early autumn of 1914 as part of the BEF where they were joined by the 1st Battalion which had been serving in India since 1904. A battalion usually consisted of 750–800 men. It was made up of four companies, each numbering about 200 men. Each company consisted of four platoons, identified by just a single letter of the alphabet. Realizing that many more men would be needed to fulfil Kitchener's initial call for 600,000 new recruits, the Lord Mayor of Manchester made plans for a new City Battalion to be formed from 'the clerks and warehousemen of the city's commercial businesses'. Initially these potential recruits had not been enthusiastic about enlisting in the existing service battalions but the idea of enlisting with friends, acquaintances and fellow workers was appealing and very successful. There were recruitment offices at the town hall and the Artillery Headquarters in Ardwick, an eastern suburb bordering on the city centre, and at the Free Trade Hall on Peter Street. By September 1,200–1,500 men were enlisting daily. The 1st City Battalion was formed in one day on 1 September. The 2nd Battalion was formed the following day and they became known as the 'Pals Battalions'. In total there would be eight Pals Battalions formed from City of Manchester men. Each battalion consisted of the standard four companies and they paraded at the Artillery Drill Hall in Ardwick. Football matches and theatres made good potential recruiting centres where large numbers of men were clustered together who would encourage each other and no-one would want to be seen holding back.

Vesta Tilley, a well-known music hall star of the time, appeared at the Palace Theatre in Manchester wrapped in a large Union Jack and singing patriotic songs. Her real name was Matilda Alice Powles and she took her stage name from Tilley, a shortened form of her name used as a nickname, and Vesta appropriately enough from the Roman goddess of hearth and home. However, Charles Scott and the *Manchester Guardian* had not finished with their protests despite controversy among some of their senior reporters. The chief leader writer, Charles Montagu, joined up, while John Hobson, the reporter who had covered the Boer War, played a large role in the anti-war movement. Scott rejected the claim that it was England's duty 'to uphold the balance of power in Europe' and criticized the initial government silence about entering the war. He wrote a letter saying 'what a monstrous and truly hellish thing this war will be if it really

Oxford Road, Manchester, *c.*1919.

brings the rest of Europe into it. It ought to sound the death knell of all autocracies – including that of our own Foreign Office.'

The Defence of the Realm Act (DoRA) was passed on 8 August, just four days after the commencement of war. In essence it gave the government unlimited powers to do whatever they saw fit for the defence of the country. Initial restrictions were understandable and comprehensible in the interests of defence and conservation:

- no public discussion or spreading of rumours concerning military or naval matters
- no trespass on railway lines or railway bridges
- no purchase of binoculars allowed
- no bonfires or fireworks allowed
- no melting down of gold or silver
- the government could take over any factory, houses, land or livestock required
- the government could censor newspapers or any other forms of communication,

afterwards descending more into the realms of 'Boy's Own farce' with additions such as:

- no one was allowed to use invisible ink when writing abroad
- no kites were to be flown
- no church bells were to be rung
- no whisky or brandy to be sold in railway refreshment rooms, although all other alcohol was available
- no bread to be fed to horses or chickens or any other animal.

The question of the drink problem also loomed large for Manchester at a very early stage of the war. Although it had long been the custom for sailors to receive a daily ration of rum many were vociferously against this tradition being extended to those serving in the Army. 'The physical efficiency and mental equilibrium of the men' was at risk of being wasted by alcohol. The city of Manchester had a severe problem with alcohol abuse and there were calls for limitation of pub opening hours while Temperance societies pleaded for total prohibition. Since the summer Russia had prohibited the production and sale of vodka and France had done the same with absinthe. Germany refused to supply its troops with alcohol and Italy had cut back. It was admitted by the government that Britain had done far less than the other nations to curb drinking of alcohol. Annual spending on drink exceeded £3,000,000 (£259,600,000 today), money badly needed to support the war. Alcohol consumption, however, was not the only problem the city faced.

If the men of the millscapes had a hard life, their womenfolk had an even harder time. Cooking, cleaning, washing, childbearing and child care also fell to their lot in addition to working in the mills. Many died young, exhausted, demoralized and desperate to escape a life that amounted to little more than slavery. It was hardly surprising that Manchester should see the birth of the Women's Social and Political Union (WSPU), a considerably more militant offshoot of the movement for the enfranchisement of women. It was led by Emmeline Pankhurst, the wife of a local doctor, and her daughters, Christabel and Sylvia. Unusually for the times, her husband was very sympathetic to the cause and lent his support. They lived at 62 Nelson Street on the western edge of Ardwick and their home was the centre of the suffragette movement. In 1914 women could not vote. They had few rights and could not take control of their own affairs if they were married. They were mostly excluded from higher education, career choices were extremely limited and they were paid far less than

Emmeline Pankhurst with her daughters Christabel and Sylvia *c.*1914. (*Courtesy of Manchester Central Library Local Studies Collection*)

men. However, despite the inequalities, unfairness and injustice suffered by all women, the minute war was declared the suffragettes (including the WSPU) unanimously suspended all activities for their own cause and threw their weight behind the common cause of fighting the enemy, offering support and hard work wherever it was needed. They cooked, cleaned, sewed 'comforts' for the soldiers, helped to care for the wounded and looked after Belgian refugees. It was the beginning of a monumental gesture which the government would recognize in full at the end of the war.

Belgian refugees had been flooding into the country from the start of the war as the German army smashed its way across their country, destroying everything and everyone in its path. In September 1914 the government offered these tragic victims of war 'the hospitality of the British nation' and undertook to provide for their 'reception, maintenance and registration'. This responsibility was delegated to local authorities who in turn delegated it to local organizations and individuals within their own areas. Many refugees were cared for in private homes but some were housed in specially-designated centres, a major one of which was Neuberg (later renamed Newbury) House in Victoria Park in Rusholme near the city centre. The local papers reported that 'It was a privilege to convey the Belgian soldiers [and some civilians] to their new temporary home ... here they were received by Mrs Thorburn and a staff of nurses of whose kindness it is impossible to speak too highly'. Some idea of their hardship was given when an appeal was published: '... these patients will need a diet in which fresh fruit and vegetables will play a prominent part as for the last two months they have subsisted on tinned meat stuffs and service biscuits ... Mrs Thorburn would therefore welcome gifts of fruit and vegetables, also tea, sugar and general groceries ... '. In addition, local Belgian refugee associations raised funds for food, clothing and rental expenses. As soon as they had recovered and also learned basic English, most Belgians found work and moved on, making way for other patients and refugees. They would remain in Britain for the duration of the Great War before returning to their own country to try and rebuild what had been lost.

There was a large Italian quarter in Ancoats. Numbers of poor Italian farmers had emigrated from their home villages during the latter half of the nineteenth century, attracted by the opportunities for work in the industrial millscapes of Manchester. Many settled in Ancoats and it was there in the 1890s that the Italian ice cream industry began. Refrigerators came into existence at around the same time and ice cream became a delicious sweet treat for both children and adults alike. Ice cream manufacture was usually a family business and the product would be made in private homes and the different families competed against each other for trade. In addition the Italians made figurines, musical instruments and barometers, plus they were also skilled craftsmen and tilers. Italy was not on the enemy side during the war, so the Italian immigrants retained relative freedom of movement and trade, although many were worried about their families in Italy whose northern borders were boxed in by the Central Powers of Germany and Austria.

Cotton production in Manchester had been steadily declining and this was now being exacerbated by skilled cotton workers enlisting in the Army. Business at the warehouses in the city centre had been sluggish over the summer due to unease over the situation in Europe and the threat of war followed by the outbreak of hostilities did little to revive it. The whole cotton manufacturing industry had been badly affected by the American Civil War and it had never really fully recovered. The mill chimneys of Ancoats, Ardwick, Hulme and Chorlton-on-Medlock were still smoking but with reduced output. However, the last few months of 1914 provided an unexpected swansong for the industry because the government needed thousands of uniforms in khaki or blue serge for all its new recruits. Suddenly the warehouses were buzzing again and 1914 turned out to be the year with highest turnover for cotton manufacture in its history. After the uniforms came the tents required which were made from army duck canvas. It might have been expected that Manchester would benefit from these requirements throughout the war but lack of skilled workers, a reduction in the supply of raw materials, the coal shortages (caused by miners enlisting) and requirements from the Front, meant this simply did not happen.

On 15 October, just before nine in the evening, the citizens of Manchester were startled by a brilliant light in the sky followed immediately by a loud bang. There was initial panic because it was believed that an airship was attacking them but Manchester Corporation's Godlee Observatory was quick to reassure them that there was no airship. It was, they insisted, a meteor falling to earth which had exploded. No one was hurt and there were no reports of damage anywhere.

On the tram posters:

JANNOCK — YOUR SHARE

ARE YOU FIGHTING OR ONLY Singing FOR RULE BRITTANIA

BOOK at the MANOR HOUSE FOR BERLIN

MORE MEN — SHORTER WAR | JOIN NOW — as a — VOLUNTEER | IT IS NOW YOUR TURN

THERE IS NO HONOUR in being COMPELLED

Tram with recruitment poster in Manchester, 1915. (*Courtesy of Manchester Central Library Local Studies Collection*)

From 1903 horse buses and trams had been gradually phased out in Manchester and replaced by steam or electric trams. Manchester Corporation opened a tram shed on Hyde Road which could accommodate 265 tramcars and introduced double-decker trams. In 1913 all-night tram services began in Manchester and the first trolley buses came into operation. Tram wires and pillars criss-crossed the city like huge mechanical spiders' webs. Although Manchester Corporation tramways carried over 200 million passengers in 1914, the advent of the Great War prevented further tramway expansion. The Corporation was also proud of their eight new Daimler motor buses. Motorized transport was the way to go. However, it was soon back to square one as the military authorities quickly requisitioned all of them, which then had to be quickly replaced by the old horse buses. Not everyone was displeased. There were those who had hated the noise and the smell of engine fumes. Horses were at least silent by comparison, if not exactly fume-free.

Initially it had been generally expected, even in Manchester, that the war would be a short, sharp lesson for the Germans and that it would all be over before Christmas with an Allied victory and all soldiers safely back home. Therefore, Manchester did not consider it necessary to establish a separate military hospital. Manchester Royal Infirmary, which stood on the site of what is now Piccadilly Gardens, had sufficient beds, or so it was believed. It quickly became apparent, however, that a military hospital was needed and it was decided, owing to the size of the city and its proximity to Liverpool (which also had a major military hospital, the 1st Western General Hospital) that the 2nd Western General Military Hospital with 520 beds should be established, and the Central High School for Boys on Whitworth Street was commandeered as its base. But even this was woefully inadequate. By the end of 1914 some 843 beds had been provided, often by the Red Cross, in auxiliary and civil buildings including Heald Place School in Rusholme (now known for its famous 'Curry Mile'), Neuberg House on Daisy Bank Road in Victoria Park, Ducie Avenue School in Whitworth Park, and the Elizabeth Gaskell School of Domestic Economy on the High Street (Hathersage Road). These were only the city area hospitals. There were also a number in other suburbs, notably Fallowfield and Didsbury. The war hospital clothing supply rooms were centred at Dower House on Oxford Road. There was a bandage room, garment room, linen room and slipper room which would supply nearly 200,000 men by the end of the war. The number of hospitals eventually grew to 113 in total, providing 3,383 extra beds for military use. Even this would stretch resources. By January 1915 well over 8,000 wounded men from the BEF had been admitted to Manchester hospitals, brought from Southampton on fifty-nine ambulance trains,

The YMCA decided to use its experience and resources to support servicemen and did that in the form of providing rest and recreational facilities. Appeals were launched to fund the building of large wooden huts for this purpose. By October over 400 marquees had been erected in Britain as a stop-gap measure but the YMCA were also establishing a number of centres in France. These numbered over 300 by 1918. They were staffed by mainly female volunteers and facilities included providing writing materials, libraries, religious services, concerts, dancing, lectures and a canteen. There were YMCA hostels in Manchester in St Georges Parish on Peter Street and at Piccadilly. The symbol of the YMCA is a red triangle representing man's body, mind and spirit, and music played a major role in reaching these parts. Bands and choirs were formed and concert parties were

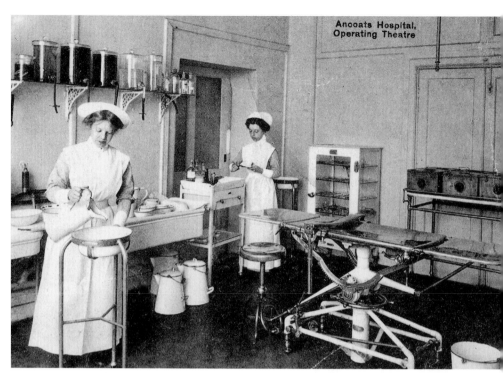

Operating theatre at Ancoats Hospital, *c.*1914 . (*Courtesy of Manchester Central Library Local Studies Collection*)

Red Cross Hospital, Manchester *c.*1914. (*Courtesy of Manchester Central Library Local Studies Collection*)

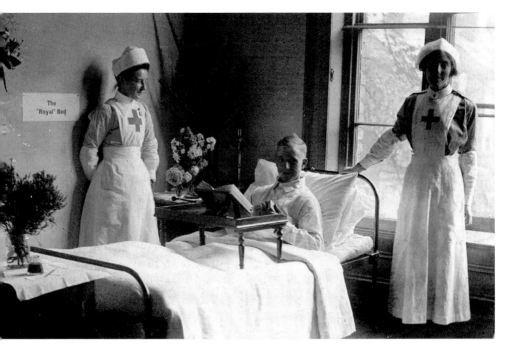

Willow Bank Military Hospital, Moss Lane East, Manchester. (*Courtesy of Manchester Central Library Local Studies Collection*)

popular. The actress Lena Ashwell was prominent in establishing concert party groups which gave over 50,000 concerts on the Western and Eastern Fronts, on troopships, and at home in Britain where Sunday afternoon concerts were popular. Entertainments arranged for wounded servicemen would often consist of a concert in public gardens or a municipal hall followed by a tea which consisted not only of the drink but included sandwiches and cakes or bread and jam.

Trading figures were now giving cause for concern, especially those for sugar and cotton. Cotton imports had fallen heavily. Towards the end of each year manufacturers normally imported much of the following year's supply but in November this year 'we only took one third the amount of American that we did in 1912 and considerably less than half the year's supply' and there was a corresponding drop in exports through loss of the German trade, which affected 50 per cent of yarn exports, and the trade in 'piece goods' with India, China, Turkey, Egypt and Argentina also fell steeply. Trade in woollen goods also declined and so did exports of iron, steel and coal. In addition, the aniline dye manufacturers and users were also experiencing problems due to Germany having largely controlled the industry before the war but it was now a hostile power and restrictions on free trade were being discussed. The idea of imposing sanctions and taxes was designed to raise money for the war effort but would have a

Piccadilly, Manchester, *c.*1904.

disastrous effect on the trade, although lack of foresight by investment capitalists was blamed as well for the current situation.

The first Christmas of the war was a time of mixed emotions in Manchester. It was now obvious that the war would not be over any time soon but many did not envisage it continuing for another whole year. Despite restrictions and hardships, efforts were made to give the children and the wounded soldiers a good Christmas. Lots of children had been bitterly disappointed at the cancellation of the traditional fireworks to celebrate Guy Fawkes Night and were looking forward to Christmas. Most children's toys had been made in Germany but trade had practically ceased with the declaration of war. However, for those who could afford to buy them, there was a good choice because there were stocks of toys which had already been imported. A new board game called 'Dash to Berlin' was, unsurprisingly, very popular; and there were still plenty of dolls for girls and tin soldiers or toy boats for boys. Carol concerts were held although the traditional bells ringing out on Christmas morning were silenced. Parcels of Christmas foodstuffs, such as plum puddings and fruit cakes, and comforts (hand-sewn or knitted garments like scarves, mufflers, gloves, pyjamas and underwear) were sent to the troops. They also each received a tin of tobacco and cigarettes from Princess Mary, the only daughter of King George V and Queen Mary. A large number of

Piccadilly, Manchester, *c.*1915.

soldiers at the Front had to make do with Maconochies' tinned stew
for their Christmas lunch but at home a typical Christmas lunch
would consist of roast pork, boiled or mashed potatoes and parsnips
followed by a plum (usually dried fruit) pudding with a hot sweet
sauce. Then there would be games and singing until teatime. Bread
and butter, tea and fruit cake would be served for tea. The most popular presents, for those who could afford them were tin soldiers for
boys and nicely-dressed dolls for girls. In the poorest households
there might be no treats but schoolchildren and those in the workhouse would be given an orange each. Few Christmas parties were
held, but, as usual, the pubs would be doing a roaring trade, although
there was a general subdued air because of so many missing faces.

CHAPTER 2

1915

At the instigation of the King, intercessionary services were held in all churches on the first Sunday of the New Year with everyone hoping that the war would end soon. Some asked how God could allow such a terrible thing but 'the world drama was laid bare ... and we got a sight of the looms of God at work'. It was said that 'we had been angry, had hated fiercely, we had resented the impeccable slanders and we had flung back words, and had exulted in the loss and sufferings of the foe and been callous at others' deaths and had a strong desire for revenge ... we had counted our gains ... after the war and gloated over the fact that our eastern competitors had been expelled from the eastern seas ...' while the clergy explained that 'Gethsemane gave the conditions to all the work of God'.

Meanwhile it was the problems in the cotton industry which remained dominant in Manchester. The loss of trade with Germany and the Near East was initially offset by the demand for service uniforms but rapidly-rising costs of raw materials and dyes, as well as reduced supplies of American and Egyptian cotton, took their toll. America was neutral and was still supplying Germany and Austria with cotton at this time but the Manchester Chamber of Trade and Commerce initially appeared confident that they would see the crisis through. They had issued a memorandum on 'Why Great Britain is at War', designed to correct misinformation about British policy in respect of Empire dependencies and neutral countries. It was published in a number of languages and a total of 135,800 copies were ordered. As always, however, the main emphasis of negotiations concerned profits. It was admitted that the 'inconvenience of dependence on Germany for so much of the materials used in dyeing and printing has been clearly brought out ...', although the situation was in fact rather more serious. For the past thirty years India, China, Japan and America had been buying up British cotton manufacturing machinery and the 'ringing of the tills' with their consequent profits

had deafened misgivings and failed to alert cotton machinery manufacturers to the real reason for the purchases which was that these
countries intended to establish their own cotton manufacturing
industries.

A nationwide problem was the supply of grain for bread. At this
point Germany was fairly self-sufficient but there was a great shortage of wheat in Britain. This was offset to some extent by a surplus of
rye but rye bread was not very popular. Barley was also becoming in
short supply. As barley is used in the making of beer, it was becoming
'a choice between beer or bread'. The effect of course was rising prices
for all types of grain which were deeply resented, especially in places
like Manchester which had fought for the repeal of the punitive Corn
Laws in the nineteenth century so that even the poor could afford to
eat bread. However, the population seemed determined to appear
intransigent when it came to accepting different types of bread in the
same way that they were resistant to eating sugar manufactured from
sugar beet (which could be home-grown) rather than cane sugar
(which had to be imported). Prices of bacon and milk were also rising,
although food shortages had not really begun to bite. There were
queues at some shops in the city for commodities in scarcer supply,
especially for those who insisted on white bread, and an unpleasant
phenomenon in the form of profiteers had begun to appear. Dried
goods could be withheld until prices were forced up and, with the
coming of refrigeration in the nineteenth century, so too could meat
supplies. The first home refrigerators had become available in 1913.
Initially this affected the poorer classes more than the better-off
but soon everyone was 'feeling the pinch'. Hoarding food was also a
problem since those with money could afford to overstock on foodstuffs leaving a reduced supply for those not so fortunate. In the millscapes of Manchester this meant some severe hardship. Even the
cost of a limited diet was becoming prohibitive. The government
requested that those who were better off should buy the more expensive cuts of meat so that poorer folk could afford a little of the
cheaper meat. This fell on deaf ears and so too did the proposal that
those who earned higher salaries should not buy potatoes because
they were the staple food of the poor. Troops at the Front also faced
a limited diet. A young subaltern wrote home that army rations
consisted of five chief items: biscuits, cheese, jam, tinned meat ('bully'
beef which was corned beef, or Maconochie's meat stew) and tea. The
biscuits were 'either whitish brown with no particular taste or brown

and crackly [with] a taste of porridge and brown sugar'. The latter were often eaten on their own but the former would be eaten with a slice of corned beef or cheese (a plain dark yellow cheese similar to Cheddar although the men would have preferred Gorgonzola) or spread with jam. Apart from raspberry and strawberry jams, the most popular varieties were apricot, greengage or plum and apple. Jam was issued in 1lb (0.5kg) tins and was supposed to serve seven men. In practice, once a tin was opened, everyone joined in until it was empty.

Marks & Spencer's Penny Bazaar, Manchester. (*Courtesy of Manchester Central Library Local Studies Collection*)

This eliminated the difficulty of having to carry half-empty tins of jam as well as the open tin being mistaken for a hand grenade in the heat of battle. This happened on a few occasions and more than one astonished German soldier found himself suddenly covered in sticky jam.

At Eastertime the majority of Mancunians were temporarily diverted from the immediate problems of war by a serious scandal which had developed on their own doorstep. Although playing football was generally encouraged as a healthy outdoor pursuit which would keep young men fit, the Football League intended to suspend professional football matches after the end of the 1914–15 season due to the war. This move would interrupt, and possibly end, the footballing careers of those playing league matches. On Good Friday, Manchester United were due to play Liverpool at Old Trafford. Liverpool were a 'mid-table team' but United were struggling to avoid relegation from the First Division. United won the game 2-0 with the same player scoring both goals, but the referee and a number of fans noted Liverpool's lack of commitment to the match and were astounded when they missed a penalty. After the match it was discovered that large amounts of money had been placed as bets at odds of 7/1 on United winning 2-0. A subsequent investigation revealed that three Manchester United players and four Liverpool players had rigged the match simply for financial gain. All seven players were banned for life by the Football Association, although after the war most of the bans were rescinded. The whole episode became retrospectively known as the 1915 British football betting scandal.

1915 saw the emergence of one of the stranger stories of the war, in which Manchester played a key part when eighteen 'moles' from the city helped to change the course of the war. These moles were not the little short-sighted furry creatures which scurry about underground messing up pristine lawns and sports greens. They were eighteen Manchester tunnellers made redundant by the sudden cessation of work on a sewer renewal contract in the city. Within four days they found themselves co-opted into the Royal Engineers and working in France. Since December 1914 the Germans had been digging shallow tunnels under 'No Man's Land', which lay between the trenches of the opposing sides, filling them with explosives and exploding the mines underneath the Allied lines. In retaliation, by March 1915, the British had eight tunnelling companies operating in Flanders. Many of the workers were from coalmining communities and there is no doubt they worked hard but progress was slow, mainly due to the heavy blue clay soil. Mining had been used for centuries for such situations. King John used it when he laid siege to Rochester Castle in 1215 and the army used it in 1770 to dig defensive positions into the Rock of Gibraltar. A special battalion to be devoted to mining duties had been requested for the Western Front in early December 1914. Major John Norton-Griffiths, who had men working on sewer renewal contracts in Manchester, suggested that 'small bore tunnels could be driven by a manual technique known as clay-kicking'. This method could only be used in firm clay soils. He explained that 'the man doing the digging sat with his back supported by a wooden frame, with his feet pointing towards the cutting face. With a spade-like tool he dug out the clay, passing the spoil overhead to a mate with disposal in the rear.' These tunnelling workers were known as the Manchester 'moles' and Norton-Griffiths requested permission to take a group of them to France. Lord Kitchener was initially cautious, but, after a demonstration by Norton-Griffiths using a coal shovel from the grate in Kitchener's office, he was allowed to travel to France to put his idea to the commanders and engineers there and to test if the soil was suitable. Once there, he gave more demonstrations to the Royal Corps of Engineers, and to Army, Corps, Division and Brigade headquarters. The clay-based soil in the Flanders region was eminently suitable for the technique. Together with Field Marshal Sir John French, the Commander-in-Chief of the BEF, and Brigadier George Fowke, the Engineer-in-Chief, Norton-Griffiths set out the structure of the tunnelling companies for which moles were adopted as a symbol in tribute to his men. On his return to Britain Norton-Griffiths insisted that, in order to speed up the formation of the companies, civilians would need to be recruited who would not have time to undergo basic military training before being deployed to the front line. Kitchener, although somewhat sceptical and reluctant, agreed because of the acute necessity to get operations under way. On Thursday, 18 December, Norton-Griffiths went immediately to Manchester and ceased the operations on one sewer contract, making eighteen staff redundant. The redundant Manchester men were then sent to Chatham on the same day to be enrolled and kitted out as Royal Engineers and by the following Monday they were tunnelling underground at Givenchy on the Western Front. Soon others joined them. A 'clay-kicking' team usually had three men: 'a "kicker" who worked at the clay face; a "bagger" who filled sandbags with lumps of clay spoil; and a "trammer" who transported the bags away by means of a small rubber-tyred trolley on rails'. Conditions were cold and cramped. Shifts could range from six to twelve hours. The tunnels were small, dark and often flooded. Many of the tunnellers at the Front suffered badly from trench foot, malnutrition and fatigue, despite a daily rum ration. A major problem was the carbon monoxide given off as a result of exploding shells and bullets. Consequently 'miners' friends', such as mice and small birds, like canaries, who were very susceptible to gas, were placed in the tunnels. If they became unconscious it was essential for the miners to evacuate immediately. Many of these hapless little animals died but a number survived and recovered once on the surface. One company kept careful records so that their little birds suffered no more than three 'gassings' before 'being pensioned off to an aviary'. Despite everything, tunnelling casualties were high and skilled volunteers were hard to replace. During one particularly bad six-week period one tunnelling company had sixteen fatalities, forty-eight casualties in hospital and eighty-six minor injuries. Another suffered twelve deaths from gas, twenty-eight in hospital and sixty minor injuries within the space of a month. After these disasters mine safety training was instigated and more mining rescue equipment was urgently requested. By 1916 essential mine rescue equipment was listed as: ten electric miner's lamps, six canaries, four mobile cages, one saw, one hand axe, three life-lines, two mine stretchers, one trench stretcher, one Primus stove, two tins of café au lait, six hot water bottles and six blankets. It was inevitable with so much tunnelling activity on both sides that there would be breakthroughs into each other's tunnels. When this occurred there was often 'vicious hand to hand fighting in the dark with picks, shovels and wood used as weapons'. The advantages of the 'clay-kicking' method was that it was an almost silent method of tunnelling, which made it difficult to detect, and it was four times as quick as the enemy's digging. British positions were also generally in lower-lying areas than those of their German counterparts which meant that they were closer to the blue clay base layer without needing to shift tons of topsoil to reach it. The Manchester men who pioneered the clay-kicking tunnelling process in the Great War are not remembered individually outside their families but a grateful France erected memorials to all the tunnellers who worked her land and played such an important part in the war.

In July, women's war agricultural committees were established to encourage females to work on the land. For several months Christabel Pankhurst had been calling for women to be allowed to do war work as well as undertaking nursing duties, caring for refugees and sewing comforts for the troops. Her belief, she said, 'was born of the realisation that the German attack on Europe is the most deadly attack that civilisation has ever sustained at the hands of barbarism, scientific or otherwise ... besides to see the magnificent working of universal war service in France ... and ... it is ... far more democratic than the practice of voluntaryism ... and also the most effective means of keeping in check the selfishness of employers, workers or any other class ...'. David Lloyd George, now Minister of Munitions, agreed with her, saying that '... in France a vast amount of work in the way of turning out shells, and especially the delicate work of fuse-making, is done by female labour ...'. Subsequently, both were delighted when the House of Commons announced in June that the National Register for War Work would include women as well as men. Christabel added that 'it is agony to think what women could have done and have not been allowed to do since the beginning of the war'. Britain had not helped the war effort by the sheer amount of prejudice it had against its own womenfolk, the insistence that females could not cope with what was seen as 'men's work' (i.e. most gainful or decently-paid employment), being only equipped for either domestic work or the most menial and low-paid of tasks. The Munitions War Act, passed in July, regulated wages, hours and conditions in the munitions industry for both sexes. The Act also made it an offence to leave employment at 'a controlled establishment', such as a munitions factory, since a number of people, mainly young men, were taking these jobs to escape military service by working for the war effort, and then leaving as soon as they decently could to obtain jobs of their choice. The result in the city of Manchester was 'a massive mobilization of the urban workforce ... helping production for the war effort'. Fitters, millwrights, machine hands, skilled or unskilled labour were required for the 'vital necessities of ... armament factories'. Women still had few personal rights, however. In the years before the war it was considered illegal for a man to beat his children or his dog but perfectly legally acceptable for him to beat his wife. Although Parliament, out of sheer necessity, had now decreed that women should be on a more equal footing and might legally do 'men's work' and/or war work, a general contempt remained for female abilities in any field outside the home, nursing or teaching, and it was not going to disappear overnight.

The Gallipoli campaign, also known as the Dardanelles, began at the end of April 1915 and lasted until the beginning of 1916. The British failed to recognize that the Ottoman army was highly trained and efficient, believing instead that it relied on undisciplined and amateur guerrilla warfare. Casualties rose to over 250,000 and it ended in a resounding victory for the Ottoman Empire. The First Lord of the Admiralty Winston Churchill (who would go on to lead Britain in the Second World War) was largely blamed for the failure of the campaign and relieved of his post. Despite the numbers of Australian, Canadian, Indian and New Zealand troops fighting on behalf of Britain, such losses detracted from resources available to fight on the Western Front and replacement of this lost manpower became a matter of urgency.

Recruitment in Manchester was continuing to respond well to Lord Kitchener's pointing finger and his plea that 'Your Country

Soldiers marching in Manchester, *c.*1914. (*Courtesy of Manchester Central Library Local Studies Collection*)

Needs You'. The numbers signing up were, at one point, greater than those for the whole of Scotland. Eight City battalions were raised as well as a public schools battalion. The latter, for which Mr J.L. Paton, the headmaster of Manchester Grammar School, was much praised, saw 800 recruits from the School's old boys joining 'the Colours'. Manchester Corporation saw some 3,000 of its eligible employees, who represented 40 per cent of the workforce, joining up and Manchester University (the Victoria University on Oxford Road) played its part as well. There were fifty-seven cadets from its Officer Training Corps in the BEF sent to relieve Belgium and France and another 346 commissions were granted to Corps members. A total of fifty-two staff and 390 students enrolled initially, but over 600 members of the Victoria University of Manchester and the Manchester Municipal School of Technology (now known as UMIST, the University of Manchester Institute of Science and Technology) had lost their lives by the end of the war. One of the most prominent and promising was Henry Moseley, a talented young physicist who worked on 'measuring the X-ray spectra of chemical elements by diffraction in crystals'. As a result he discovered 'a relationship between wavelength and atomic number' which became known as Moseley's Law. He was killed by a sniper at Gallipoli on 10 August 1915. Engineering recruits were in short supply and urgently needed, but electrical and mechanical engineers from the School of Technology 'developed a deep-sea hydrophone to counter the submarine threat to shipping ... a high frequency alternator to power aircraft radios was produced, and the materials used to construct aircraft were routinely tested in the Textiles Department'. In addition 'a new type of gas furnace was designed for the heat treatment of tool steels ... increasing the rate at which shells could be machined ... and metallurgists produced cast iron of high tensile strength, enabling the range of gas shells to be doubled'. Instruments were manufactured to measure permeability in airship fabrics and the 'envelopes of both the *R33* and *R34* airships were treated with "dope" to strengthen the fabric'. Research was also done to improve war materials and substitutes for materials in short supply.

Many of those enlisting from the inner-city millscapes of Manchester saw the chance to serve their country not only as a patriotic duty but as a chance to escape the life of drudgery in often squalid conditions that many of them knew. Another factor was the chance for male domestic servants to escape an often badly-paid life of servitude and second-class citizenship. As soon as female labour was required for war work and to do the jobs previously only done by men, female domestic servants also deserted their posts in droves. This happened all over the country as well as in Manchester and it was an unexpected consequence of the war that the Victorian and Edwardian country house way of life, depicted so well by *Downton Abbey*, was virtually destroyed.

Businesses in Manchester also suffered badly from loss of staff as well as loss of trade and unpaid invoices from now-hostile powers. Banking Clearing House reports had shown a loss of £43,000,000 (£3,108,000,000), representing 12.9 per cent, from August to December 1914. This was greater than anywhere else, even London, which had only experienced an 11 per cent loss. Nevertheless, the City of Manchester was managing to meet all the military and commercial demands made upon it and proudly announced that a total of £180,000 (£13,010,000) had been raised for various relief funds. Citizens imposed a voluntary tax on themselves: £86,970 (£6,285,000) was received of which £51,167 (£3,698,000) was spent on the local relief fund. £100,000 (£7,227,000) had also been given 'in kind' and to the soldiers' comforts funds in addition to £20,000 (£1,445,000) for the Belgian Relief Fund (800 Belgian refugees were now resident in the City and homes for another 2,000 were funded by the City), as well as £10,000 (£722,700) for the wounded and refugees.

The 'gallant Manchesters' were receiving much praise, although by the end of March 1915 a total of 10,000 men from the BEF had been treated at Manchester General Western Hospital and by the local Red Cross. Hospital trains arrived daily from Southampton and medical staff worked non-stop to treat the wounded soldiers or at least alleviate their suffering. The trains were equipped with wards, an operating theatre, medical quarters, a pharmacy, canteen, bathrooms and recreational facilities. On arrival the walking wounded could help themselves to some extent but those who could not walk were laid on stretchers in low rows on the station platform waiting for ambulance transport. Red Cross teams worked round the clock to welcome and assist the injured and then take them to hospital. The Pasteur Institute in Paris had made a breakthrough in early March in the quest for a serum to treat gangrene. It could hardly have come at a better time and it was hoped that arrangements could soon be made to supply the Army Medical Service with as much serum as required. Chlorine gas was first unleashed by the Germans at the Battle of

Ypres on 22 April. Chlorine is an element used by the dyeing industry and it is also the basis for bleaches. Used in small quantities it is safe, kills harmful bacteria and is used in swimming pools to keep the water clean. Occasionally a little too much is used and swimmers complain of sore throats and stinging eyes. In the Great War chlorine gas was used in large and lethal quantities as a weapon, initially by the Germans. The gas corrodes mouth, nose, eyes, throat and lungs, causing chemical burns and irreversible damage, and many soldiers died prolonged and agonizing deaths. This caused much bitterness among front-line Allied troops who saw their comrades die in such a dreadful fashion and the tone of the fighting began to change. Horrified and disbelieving soldiers wrote home about what they had seen and anti-German feeling increased rapidly on the home front. Anyone with a German-sounding name, even if a naturalized British citizen, ran the risk of attack, and German-owned businesses were looted. Manchester was acutely aware of the numbers of wounded soldiers and the terrible conditions at the Front from those treated by the General Western Hospital. A plea had been made for funding for a soup kitchen by a nurse working at the Front whose husband was in the Lancaster Regiment. She had named the project 'The Lancashire Lasses Soup Kitchen' and she wanted a motorized soup kitchen to supply soup, tea, cocoa and coffee to the wounded at the Front line after they had received first aid. The city of Manchester businessmen and mill-owners promptly put their hands in their collective pockets and obliged.

The sinking of the *Lusitania* on 7 May off the southern coast of Ireland with the loss of nearly 1,200 lives caused outrage everywhere. The *Manchester Guardian* called it a terrible crime which had awoken very bitter feelings against Germany. There were two recorded explosions and the ship sank rapidly after the second one. The Germans were roundly censured for torpedoing a civilian ship carrying women and children but they retorted that the ship had been carrying ammunition and was therefore classed as a naval warship. They also stated that only one torpedo was fired which could not account for the two explosions and rapid sinking of the ship. Their accusations were hotly refuted and several post-war governments insisted that the *Lusitania* had simply been a civilian passenger ship. Anti-German demonstrations took place in Manchester and there were several attacks on shops, businesses and people who were perceived to be German. There was also rioting in Liverpool, which had lost a number of its citizens in the tragedy, and retribution was demanded. German nationals living in Britain were advised to loudly and publicly condemn what was seen as an act of pure barbarism on the part of the Fatherland. It seemed, initially, that even the Kaiser was shocked for he suspended unrestricted submarine warfare in September although he relaxed this restriction about eighteen months later. However, it was discovered that this move originated more from a desire to keep America out of the war rather than any finer feelings about the numbers of drowned humanity. The sting in the tail is that in recent years (first decade of the twenty-first century) divers have discovered that the *Lusitania* had indeed been carrying a large amount of ammunition and the civilian nature of the ship had been used by both British and American authorities as a cover for the ship's real cargo.

There was an acute shortage of shells and ammunition due both to the heavy fighting and Kitchener's underestimation of the firepower that would be required. Lloyd George had been appointed Minister of Munitions in May and he quickly discovered that not only was there an acute shortage of ammunition but the country was actually spending more on alcohol than munitions. Canon Green had given an address on the acute problems caused by drink to the Manchester diocesan Church of England Temperance Society in the Town Hall on 9 March, and he had wondered 'whether the average Englishman or Englishwoman had any conception of the word enjoyment apart from strong drink'. An angry Lloyd George put it more bluntly. 'We are fighting Germany, Austria and drink, and as far as I can see, the greatest of these three deadly foes is drink.' He was determined to put an end to the situation and under the terms of DoRA he took action. Licensing hours were to be reduced from 19 hours to 5.5 hours per day and he added a 'No Treating Order' which meant people could not buy a round of drinks so that better-off drinkers could no longer buy a drink for their poorer friends. The only exception allowed to no treating would be that if someone was hosting a lunch or dinner in a restaurant, then it would be permissible to pay for drinks for guests as part of the meal. Naturally there was outrage, mostly from pubs, but Lloyd George stuck to his guns, and Manchester publicans began to think laterally. The pubs had not been ordered to close, but they could only sell alcohol during the designated 5.5 hours. So they remained open. In the morning tea, coffee and hot Bovril were sold to workers and shoppers. At lunchtime mugs of soup were added to the liquid menus and after 9.30pm, when alcohol sales ceased, cocoa was sold as a warming bedtime drink. People could still gather to socialise or to play dominoes and backgammon. The restaurants faced more of a problem in that patrons might buy a sandwich or a small cake, claim it was a meal, and thus they would be allowed to both drink and treat others. The *Manchester Guardian* condemned this practice with scorn. 'It seems very stupid and undignified, this obvious desire to see a tiny sandwich or a biscuit officially recognized as a "meal" merely in order to rend half useless an order which inflicts no hardship on anyone and the introduction of which met with no protest at all of any importance ... there is an uncompromising frivolity about a type of mind which accepts a principle without protest and then immediately bends its misdirected wits to considering how the application of the principle can be avoided.'

Due to lack of supplies and the loss of skilled staff through enlistment, a number of Manchester manufactories were on short-time working and some had simply closed down. Lloyd George ordered that empty or shut-down industrial buildings should be converted into munitions factories. In and around the city centre industrial buildings were mainly warehouses and the nearest munitions factory was at the Beyer Peacock foundry in the eastern suburb of Openshaw. Women were now free to apply for munitions jobs as they had been allowed to register for war work. The wages offered were much better than in the textile industry and girls flocked to offer their services. This was a further blow to those mills still working. Female conductors were employed on the trams and buses by Manchester Corporation for the first time due to staff shortages caused by enlistment although initially this was not popular with the public, especially the men. Food and fuel prices were rising steadily and it was imperative that folk earn as much as they could in order to feed and house their families. There were strikes for higher wages by those remaining in the cotton industry and the Manchester Carters' Association demanded an increase in wages and overtime rates. It was recognized that there was a difficult situation but many employers simply did not have sufficient funds to meet further wage demands, especially as a number were already paying war bonuses to cope with inflated prices. Those at the Front who read about the strikes in the *Manchester Guardian*, when it was posted out to them, were horrified. Soldiers could not strike. That would be mutiny and they would face a firing squad. They were paid far less than most and, ironically, received no war bonuses. Soldiers' dependents were also having a tough time. Despite the initial separation allowances paid by the military authorities increasing in March of 1915 they were still barely adequate. The wife of the lowest rank of private was paid 12s 6d (£45.17) per week and there were grades, according to the husband's rank, so that the wife of a warrant officer first class received 23/- (£83.11) for herself per week. An allowance of 5/- (£18.06) per week was paid for the first child and 2s 6d (£9.03) per week for the second child with 2/- (£7.22) per week payable for each subsequent child. Motherless children received 5/- (£18.06) per week each. Over half the money received in allowances was usually paid for rent; the rest had to feed and clothe the family. In addition soldiers' working conditions were cold, wet, dangerous and often knee-deep in mud, and they couldn't understand why those in the safety of the home country, who had hot meals and a proper bed in which to sleep, should even think of going on strike in wartime. Many saw it as a betrayal.

On the first anniversary of the war intercessionary services were held in local churches and several hundred wounded soldiers attended a service in Manchester cathedral. The main problem now looming large for the authorities was how to pay for the war. The *Manchester Guardian* concurred with the government in believing that the right way was through saving on a national scale. 'Saving is a national duty now', wrote the paper, 'because if we spend our money we cannot lend it to the government, which wants it for the costliest war that was ever waged.' The government was only receiving just over a quarter of what was needed through taxation. Economy was being urged in every area and self-sufficiency was being promoted. Food imports needed to be greatly reduced. Travel on public transport was to be reduced to save on coal and petrol. Trade tariffs on imports and exports were proposed, thus abandoning the principle of free trade which had long been cherished. A scheme of war loans and war bonds was devised whereby people saved any money they could and invested in the war at a relatively high interest rate of up to 5 per cent. Although this would prove to be a heavy burden on the post-war economy it solved the problem for now. War savings associations were established in many workplaces where folk could pay just a few pence a week. Every contribution counted and Lloyd George nick-named them 'Silver Bullets' since all the money would ultimately help to defeat the Kaiser. In addition the special war budget affected everyone and 'imposed additional and unprecedented burdens' on the population: 50 per cent extra duty had been levied on tea, tobacco, cocoa, coffee, chicory and dried fruits and 33.3 per cent had been levied on motorcycles, cars, cinema films, clocks, watches, musical instruments and plate glass. Luxury goods were clearly less affected, but the government, then as now, had an eye to the main chance and taxed the commodities which were popular, some would say essential, and which everyone bought. The tariffs had been hotly contested by the free trade lobby but the government needed to raise a great deal of money within a short time to continue supporting the war.

Milk prices were rising sharply as well. Although not part of city-centre life in Manchester the farmers of Lancashire and Cheshire, like their colleagues in all counties, were having an effect on every-one in the country through their general intransigence. An Australian farmer, on a lecture tour in Britain, remarked that British farmers were very resistant to change. Nowhere was this better illustrated than in their attitude to farm labour. There were labour shortages every-where which were making many aspects of everyday life difficult but in many occupations other people were learning to do the work done by those now fighting at the Front. The farmers were having none of it. They wanted their sons home from the war for ploughing and harvesting duties, stating that their skilled labour and knowledge was essential and insisting on their repatriation at sowing and reaping times. There was alternative labour available but it was rejected on various grounds. They refused to have prisoners of war on their land, although British prisoners of war worked on German farms. Irish labour was too expensive. The Boy Scouts and the older boys who could work during the school holidays were deemed too inexperi-enced, and they simply refused to either countenance or train female labour, although the wives, mothers and daughters of farmers were used to helping out with farm duties, and one 76-year-old lady insisted that she could plough a field as well as any man. Throughout 1915 the authorities had learned to accept that labour must be taken from wherever it was available but, despite the alternative sources of labour, the government found themselves in the ridiculous situ-ation of being forced to repatriate a number of farmers' sons for the harvest which was both expensive and inefficient. Lloyd George was particularly irritated and swore that if the war continued the situation would have to change. The Germans had been carrying out a cam-paign of sinking as much British merchant shipping as possible to try and starve the country into submission. Lloyd George's response was to advocate as much self-sufficiency as possible and he asked that people should use their gardens and allotments to grow potatoes, vegetables and fruit for themselves and their families plus hopefully a surplus. The City of Manchester, understanding that many of its residents did not have any access to gardens or allotments, began to consider turning its public parks and waste ground into allotments so that they could be worked by inner city dwellers who could then grow their own fresh produce.

For the first time in history aerial warfare had been unleashed and a bewildered populace were warned to expect death raining from the skies. German Zeppelins had embarked on 'a mission of murder' and their aerial bombardments were causing widespread terror on the East Coast and in East Anglia, the Home Counties and London. Invasion was now seen as a real threat. Under DoRA lighting restrictions were instituted to make it harder for the Zeppelins to see targets during night-time raids. Manchester was not in as much danger as those towns and cities on the eastern side of the country because the city lay almost at the limit of the range of the Zeppelins but all the same they represented a threat. At this point there wasn't a total blackout order due to working, trading and safety aspects, but street lamps had to be partly obscured. Manchester chose to darken the top of its street lamps so that they would be less visible from above while giving pedestrians below some much needed illumination of the streets. The nearby town of Stockport, which always kept a keen eye on what Manchester did, seemed to feel they were in competition with their neighbouring city, comparing the two places endlessly and attempting to re-assure themselves that they had done as well as, if not better, than Manchester. The lighting restriction situation descended into farce as Stockport decided how to partially obscure its street lights. The town had no option but to obey the DoRA restrictions, although they did it their way and obscured the lower part of their street lamps. Consequently people struggled and fell over in the darkened gloom of the streets while from above clusters of pretty glowing lights could be seen from afar. Manchester tried to be charitable and not to laugh but the situation prompted a local wit to comment that while Manchester was expecting attacks from Zeppelins, Stockport was clearly expecting attacks from submarines.

At the end of July, under a scheme initiated by Lord Derby for all towns and cities, the city council instigated their preliminary preparations for taking the National Register in Manchester as laid down under the terms of the National Registration Act passed that month.

This was mainly in response to the fact it was widely felt that insufficient numbers of young single men were not doing their duty and enlisting, leaving it to the generally older married men to do so. Often when older men had enlisted the younger men would step into their jobs which meant better wages. Consequently, on 15 August all men and women, aged 15 to 65 years, were to register at the address where they usually lived. This differed from a census in that each individual, and not the head of the household, had to register on their own form – 29 million forms were issued nationally for this purpose. Men had to complete a blue form and women had to complete a white one. Separate card indexes were then compiled for men and women. Indexes for both sexes were in two groups; one for single people and one for married people. Each group was sub-divided into occupations. There were forty-six groups for males and thirty groups for females. These were then sub-divided again into age groups – eight groups for men and six groups for women – before being filed alphabetically. From this information two further indexes were compiled. Pink forms were completed for all men aged 18 to 41 years and green forms for people with secondary occupations. Registration certificates were then issued to each person and recorded in a ledger. There was a £5 (£350) fine for anyone who refused to complete the forms or who gave false information. It was consequently resolved that every man not 'starred' on the pink form as being engaged in war work should be personally canvassed. They were classified by age into forty-six groups, twenty-three groups for married men and twenty-three groups for young single men. Most folk suspected that the whole exercise was simply an indirect way of discovering how many men eligible for military service had not yet enlisted and they were right. Lloyd George's concern was that there would not be sufficient voluntary enlisters and that conscription would have to be introduced at some point in the not too distant future. There was talk of military training to take place in local schools but this idea was firmly rejected by the 'high' master of Manchester Grammar School on the grounds that people were already obsessed with the war and it would do 'impressionable boys' little good, encouraging young men to believe that warfare was the solution to everything.

Some foodstuffs were in increasingly short supply and these included meat, wheat, flour and sugar. British people have long had a sweet tooth and even when sugar was rationed the weekly allowance per adult was half a pound (0.25kg) per week. However, it wasn't just sugar causing the problem; it was the type of sugar. Cubed sugar was greatly prized (hence the famous question of one lump or two) and loose granulated sugar was not. Cane sugar was definitely the sugar of preference but this had to be imported. Sugar beet, which could produce equally good sugar, could be easily grown in Britain and East Anglian soils were ideal. Thousands of arable acres all over the country had been laid waste in the farming depression towards the end of the nineteenth century and it was felt that these acres could be reclaimed for growing food and for growing sugar beet in the eastern counties. It wasn't so much resistance to this idea as dithering and prevarication which were causing the problems. Many saw it as a great opportunity for self-sufficiency and for trade after the war. Others weren't so sure. New machinery would be needed for growing and harvesting a sugar beet crop and processing plants could be expensive. British farmers had almost a Luddite approach to farming machinery and couldn't afford the expense at this point in time anyway. The government suggested farming co-operatives which would buy the machinery and then members could borrow it in turns. Financial incentives of cheap loans and grants were offered for purchasing machinery. Farmers were slow to agree and it would be another year before sugar beet cultivation really got under way. By this time food shortages were becoming more acute and the government was having to instruct on reclamation of farming land and what crops should be grown. There was a shortage of meat, partly due to the Army's requirements, partly due to the German blockade and partly due to profiteers who would hoard meat frozen in refrigerators to try and push up the price. Coal was in short supply as well. The number of miners who had enlisted had seriously affected the output from the mines and extra coal was also needed for transport of supplies and men both in Britain and at the Fronts. Carriage charges had risen too along with everything else.

As Christmas approached in Manchester there were numerous appeals for charity to give wounded soldiers and Belgian refugees some special treats, and also for the children of those serving in the armed forces. Local newspapers appealed for 'comforts' for soldiers' Christmas parcels and on 10 December Miss Violet Vanbrugh, a Shakespearean actress who had worked with Henry Irving and Ellen Terry, gave a special matinee performance at the Theatre Royal on Peter Street in aid of the Indian Soldiers' Fund. However, the sheer number of appeals for food, clothes and toys in the city and its inner

Deansgate, Manchester, *c*.1914.

suburbs illustrate how deprived life had become for some sections of the populace. The Rev. A.H. Swann of St Marks Church in Hulme requested money, clothes and toys to 'enable him to give the little ones a Christmas treat'. The rector of St Catherine's in Cheetham asked for donations to give 570 slum children a free breakfast on Christmas Day, while Grosvenor Street Baptist Church in Chorlton-on-Medlock wanted to provide their old folk with a Christmas treat. Holland Street Ragged School in Ancoats appealed for gifts of toys to be given to children and clothing for the elderly 'to brighten the many saddened homes of the district'. The Boatmen's Bethel organization in Castlefield, just off Deansgate, wrote that 'the committee desire to provide, as in past years, meals and comforts for old people and the poor children of a district in which much poverty and distress prevail ...' and appealed for clothing, boots, bedding, provisions and toys.

Thomas Ackroyd at the Boys and Girls Refugees centre in Strangeways, an area now notorious for its prison, wrote that 'he hopes to provide, as in other years, a Christmas treat and a little gift for every child ...'. The Crippled Children's Help Society, who had offices in Cross Street and Shude Hill in the city centre, were collecting money for 500 hampers to be given to the worst affected cases and gifts for 700 less severely disabled, so that 'each of the afflicted little ones confined in the homes of the Manchester and Salford poor shall receive on Christmas morning a hamper of good things', but it was the

Salvation Army in Cheetham Hill who made the most heartfelt appeal. They 'plead for some Christmas cheer for their 2,000 sorrowful and desolate protégés: for the aged, afflicted poor ... many of whom live in one room with no fire and little food ... and for the neglected little ones, poorly clad and often ill-used, who live in Slumland and are looking for Father Christmas'. The appeal continued that 'money, garments, toys, coal or food will be most gladly received.' The whole ethos was that of *A Christmas Carol*, the novel by Charles Dickens which so ruthlessly exposed the terrible price exacted by the Industrial Revolution in nineteenth-century England, the greed that wealth engendered and the pathos of thousands of crippled and malnourished children like Tiny Tim. This novel was written seventy years before the war but the appeals illustrated the continuing problems in Manchester. However, despite everything, city folk were managing to find the determination and strength to help the war effort. The Kaiser was not going to win.

CHAPTER 3

1916

A service of intercession was held in the cathedral on the first Sunday
of the New Year but it was not well attended by local folk. Although
the Dean gave an address, it was not a particular occasion for unifica-
tion. The Nonconformist ministers, all robed in black from nearby
Chetham's Hospital, sat on one side of the nave while the Anglican
clergy sat on the other side uniformly attired in surplices. One reason
for low attendance of the congregation might have been that many of
them were coping with 'widespread damage and [some] loss of life in
the cyclonic force of the wind in the fierce New Year's day gale'.

Three young children were hit and injured when a billposting
hoarding blew down in Great Ancoats Street, which resulted in one
of them being detained in hospital. A 6-year-old boy was hit on the
head by falling bricks in Worth Street, although he was not seriously
hurt, and a pensioner in Ardwick had a lucky escape when a chimney

Chetham's Hospital, Manchester, c.1910.

stack fell through the roof and landed on the bed in which he was resting. A number of slates and chimney stacks blew down, trees were felled, railway lines blocked and football matches cancelled. Manchester City and Manchester United were both playing away and, although their games went ahead, both sides lost their matches; City losing 2-0 to Blackpool while United lost 2-1 to Stoke. On a lighter note, which made Manchester residents smile, the local newspaper carried reports of a banquet for retired horses and recovering war horses. 'The banquet consisted of a liberal supply of carrots, apples, bread, biscuits and sugar and, without exception, the feeding boxes were emptied to the last morsel.'

New lighting restrictions for Manchester came into force in January. The restrictions now applied from two hours after sunset until half an hour before sunrise. It was thought that this would permit lighting for the 'busiest portions of twenty-four hours'. During the 'dark period' there were to be no headlights on motor cars and tram lights were to be dimmed with no more than two lights showing at the front. No electric light bulb was to give a light of more than twelve candlepower. Only one burner could be used in oil lamps and acetylene lamps were limited in the amount of fuel they could consume in one hour. Paper or paint was used to partially obscure external lighting. Lights inside tram cars and buses were to be shaded. Horse-drawn vehicles and bicycles had to carry a white light at the front and a red light at the rear. German Zeppelins had increased their attacks along the east coast and local authorities were anxious that their attention should not be drawn to towns and cities in their area. While the city of Manchester lay on the limits of Zeppelin range, the airships had been seen over Ashton-under-Lyne just under seven miles away. Following on from the lighting restrictions it was proposed that a form of daylight saving should be introduced in Britain to save fuel and lighting and also to encourage longer working hours. On 21 May the daylight saving Act came into force and Britain went onto what is still known as British summertime. This move was met with a few grumbles but most folk, especially the children, welcomed the longer hours of daylight.

In mid-February the *New York Tribune* published an amazing and widely disseminated interview with Walter Long, President of the Local Government Board, which demonstrated how alarmingly out of touch some people could be. Mr Long began by referring to the general absence of signs of war in Britain. He said that 'the existence of war is only revealed by ... khaki clad soldiers everywhere and ... the grim earnestness of the whole population. Everybody is working ... and pauperism shows immense signs of diminution.' He went on to say the only exceptions were the seaside towns which depended on tourism and faced regular attacks from Zeppelins. Generally, trade was brisk and the working class were earning far higher wages than ever before. He did not mention that folk were also paying more for food, fuel and in rent than ever before. Although Mr Long fully acknowledged the role that women were now playing, he went on to explain how further economies could be made and that more self-sufficiency should be encouraged. He seemed to be totally oblivious to the impact the war was having in all walks of life on all types of people and he did not appear to question why the whole population was full of 'grim earnestness'. Mr Long stated that he had 'travelled through Great Britain' before making his statements, but neither he nor the newspaper elaborated on the places he had visited. Manchester was clearly not among them and nor were many of the northern towns.

The Amalgamated Society of Engineers was holding talks with the government to safeguard pay and conditions for skilled workers. Enlistment had caused an acute shortage of skilled workers and the union was being asked to accept semi-skilled and unskilled labour in order to 'keep the wheels of industry turning'. Engineering was not the only industry to be affected. In Manchester, where the engineering and cotton industries had lost a lot of skilled and senior workers, a number of employers refused to accept women working in what were traditionally seen as men's jobs.

Trams suffered in the same way, with a hostile public initially resistant to female conductresses. Women working in shops or delivering the post suffered similar taunts and hostility. Prior to the war many married women were not supposed to do paid work, although a lot of them did, hiding their rings on chains under high-necked blouses and insisting that they were single. There was also a growing shortage of coal, due to the number of miners enlisting, so that fuel costs had been steadily rising, forcing the government to consider legislation to fix prices. In certain areas of Greater Manchester some females did mining jobs and, for the sake of safety, tied their long skirts into pantaloons. This was regarded as completely shocking by a number of folk and, such was the novelty, young men would gather to watch as these women emerged from their work. However, the government

Conductresses at Manchester Corporation tram depot, *c.*1915. (*Courtesy of Manchester Central Library Local Studies Collection*)

was now simply more interested in whether a person could actually do the job than in prejudices, bureaucracy or forms of dress, because it was both important and necessary that essential industries and occupations should be maintained. It would be easy to blame the unions for resistance but their privileges had been hard won and in any case widespread public prejudice was a much greater problem. Some of it was simply resistance to any change but slowly many learned to accept the changes; at least for the duration of the war. However, these concerns paled beside the main issue of the spring of 1916 which was conscription.

As Lloyd George had feared, the Derby Scheme of 1915 failed to produce sufficient numbers of recruits and the Military Service Act 1916 was passed on 2 March. Under the Act men aged 18 to 41 years old could be called up for army service unless they were married, widowed with children, serving in the Royal Navy, a minister of religion or working in a reserved occupation. Reserved occupations were those deemed essential for support of the war and the country such as farming, mining, transport, shipbuilding, munitions production etc. Up to this point unmarried men had fared much better than married men. Now the tables were turned and there were vociferous protests. It was a valid point that many unmarried men also had dependants and responsibilities. The government eventually admitted this fact and, in May, a supplementary Act was passed to include all men aged 18 to 41 who were medically fit for service, whether they were married or not. Local military service tribunals were set up which had the power to grant exemption from service, although in most cases this would be either temporary or conditional. Being ordered to fight for a country where large numbers of men did not have any electoral representation, for a cause that many did not really understand, was a step too far for some men and the role of conscientious objector was born. However, their refusal to fight or, on the part of a few, to help in any way with the war effort, was seen as cowardice rather than principle and most were either imprisoned or shunned or both.

There was a diversion from these problems at Easter when Irish Republicans, taking advantage of the fact that the British army was heavily engaged with the war, decided to stage an armed rebellion, known as the Easter Uprising, to end British rule so that Ireland could become an independent republic. Manchester had a large Irish immigrant population, originally centred on 'Little Ireland' in Chorlton-on-Medlock, which had spread to all parts of the city and its environs. Much of the railway, canal and reservoir construction had been done by Irish navvies. In 1914 Liam Parr and Gilbert Lynch had set up the Manchester Company of the Irish Volunteers in the city who were committed to an independent Ireland. The government had plans, shelved at the beginning of the war, for Irish home rule. It was an issue which caused bitter divisions among politicians and civilians. When the Great War broke out Parr and Lynch decided to go to Dublin and fight for Irish independence rather than fight for Britain. They were joined by Larry Ryan, a Mancunian who worked on the Ashton Canal at Meadow Street Wharfs, Piccadilly, and Redmond Cox, a grocer's assistant from Cheetham, just north of Strangeways prison. They travelled to Ireland unobtrusively early in 1916. On Easter Monday they were part of a group which took over the General Post Office building and Parr helped rebels to set up a radio station to broadcast the news of Irish independence. However the British army reacted swiftly. Rebel forces of 1,500 faced 20,000 well-trained men with much greater firepower. By this time much of Dublin was burning and this caused even greater problems and confusion. The uprising was swiftly and brutally crushed with many casualties: almost 500 deaths and over 2,600 wounded. The ringleaders of the uprising were executed but Parr, Ryan and Cox were arrested and imprisoned in Knutsford. Lynch, injured in the fighting, escaped imprisonment and returned home. It was an episode which caused great diversion and had a lasting effect on the Irish community in central Manchester, increasing their sympathy and determination for Irish independence.

The summer of 1916 changed the entire course of the war for everyone in Britain. On 5 June Lord Kitchener, whose pointing arm on recruiting posters had become such an iconic image of the Great War, drowned when HMS *Hampshire*, the warship taking him to Russia for negotiations, hit a German mine and sank off the Scottish coast. He had paid a visit to Manchester in March 1915, saluting a 'march past' of Manchester battalions, and the city was shocked by his death. Kitchener was replaced as Secretary of State for War by Lloyd George.

General Sir Douglas Haig, Commander-in-Chief of the British Expeditionary Force, masterminded the Battle of the Somme. Lloyd George was not in favour of this battle, seeing it as a great mistake, but was told firmly by Haig that, as he was not a military man, he could not possibly understand military strategy and that he should

"THE MARCH PAST."

Troops marching past Lord Kitchener in Albert Square, Manchester, 21 March 1915.
(*Courtesy of Manchester Central Library Local Studies Collection*)

not interfere. Haig was a stubborn and confident man. He told Lloyd George that the battle would last one day and that it would decisively rout the Germans. He was so sure of success that he arranged for the battle to be filmed in order that everyone could watch it and marvel at the German defeat. The date of the battle was set for 1 July. It became one of the greatest military disasters in history, lasting not one day but four and a half months. There were more than a million casualties. A vindicated Lloyd George said, after watching the film of the battle, that 'if the exhibition of this picture all over the world does not end war, God help civilisation!' The British made little progress but the introduction of tanks in the autumn of 1916, after training soldiers in their use at a secret location in Suffolk, was an important development and the sign of things to come. The war poets also stopped seeing 'the glory of war' and began to recognize the awful bloody reality of it coupled with the senseless waste of so many lives, most of them young.

Coping with the huge number of casualties from the Somme was difficult enough but Manchester also faced another medical problem in common with much of the rest of the country. Venereal diseases, more commonly known today (2016) as sexually-transmitted diseases (STDs), had become a hidden epidemic. Numbers of soldiers were returning from active service infected with syphilis or gonorrhoea and were now in danger of infecting their wives or sweethearts back home. Syphilis in particular could be fatal if not treated and often led to madness in the sufferer. Arsenic treatments and mercury-based creams were used to treat STDs because the doctors of the time did not realize the poisonous potential these treatments had. Military commanders were quick to blame women, insisting that their soldiers were 'clean and innocent', with the result that whereas free treatment was available for men without punishment, women had to pay and could also be charged with an offence, even if infected by their husbands. A former workhouse and boys' school in the city was commandeered and opened as New Bridge Street Hospital in 1916 as a specialist venereal diseases hospital, which had 530 beds. Some patients did not have other medical problems and grew restless, wanting to be out and about but this had to be forbidden for fear that contact with others would spread STDs still further.

Rapidly-increasing shortages of food and fuel and growing queues for bread, meat and sugar were causing some concern, and food prices were continuing to give grief. Many farmers blamed the shortage of available labour to milk cattle for problems with the supply of milk, saying that the animals did not respond so well to females milking them. The long-cherished image of the English milkmaid seemed to have been forgotten, although the cows doubtless saw the priority of having their udders relieved by the removal of milk as a rather higher priority than the sex of the person doing the milking. However, Cheshire farmers, along with farmers in other regions, unhappy with the low price (as they saw it) of milk were further limiting the supply by sending milk for cheese making, which gave them greater profits, or by creating artificial shortages to force up prices. There were also numerous complaints that milk was being watered down. The government, while aware that farmers should have the right to determine what they did with their own dairy products, knew that the current situation could not continue. In addition, there was disquiet that wheat was subject to profiteering by ship-owners and others in the trade, and compulsory purchase of the entire stock of home-grown wheat was being advocated. There was also concern about rising bacon prices and there were demands for a food minister to be

Queue for potatoes at Jackson's Market in Manchester, *c.*1915. (*Courtesy of Manchester Central Library Local Studies Collection*)

appointed who could introduce some kind of rationing via a ticket system. One of the problems was that some people were still eating and drinking too much and too well. While this was certainly not true of the poorer folk of Manchester, who could barely afford basic necessities, it was very true of some of the better-off citizens and Parliament itself felt that luxury goods and richer people were not sufficiently taxed and should pay a good deal more. Numbers of people were still insisting on pure butter and refused to countenance any substitutes. White bread and white cubed cane sugar were also much in demand. Vegetarians were also having a hard time. The difficulty lay not so much in acquiring extra cheese or eggs but in getting extra vegetables. The gradual scarcity of some foodstuffs resulted in long queues at butchers and grocers. If there was the slightest rumour that a certain shop had acquired extra supplies queues would form quickly. A Rusholme girl told her mother on one occasion of 'a queue outside the Maypole ... they're selling half a pound of butter ...'. Often long before a shop was open some folk sent children to queue for them from 4.00am until they went to school. It was noted that 'in the cotton areas' inferior cuts of meat were bought as frequently as the better cuts. Some butchers were having a difficult time maintaining stable prices. The problem was that no-one wanted to pay for bones – understandably customers just wanted the meat. But butchers had to buy whole carcasses, bones and all. This created a situation where they could not fully capitalize on what they bought. Some of the meatier bones would be bought for broths and soups but the remainder would be the butcher's loss. Although sugar and petrol were already rationed, some MPs felt that 'a system of bread tickets and meat coupons was harmful ... rationing ... would lead to great evils ... and we ought to avoid putting ourselves in the position of a blockaded people ...'. The writing, however, was on the wall, and on 22 December the first Ministry of Food was established. It was headed by a Food Controller, Lord Rhondda, who could regulate food production, supply and consumption.

Education had suffered too as a result of the war with schools being requisitioned as hospitals and older children undertaking some war work and more family duties. It was realized from the number of casualties to date that a new generation of skilled workers was going to be essential if the country was to survive on the world stage. The school leaving age was 14 but there was talk of raising it to 16 and there were proposals for a number of night schools so that young people who had already left school and were working could further their education. A discussion by the Lancashire and Cheshire Branch was of the Incorporation of Assistant Masters on the future of secondary education as held at Manchester Grammar School in May. The discussion was chaired by Bishop Welldon. He stated that

> after the war the European world would assume a ... disastrously novel character. It would be a bankrupt world. Many social and economic reforms ... would have to be postponed. A new feeling about the State and the individual would be created. Too much had been thought of the individual and too little of the State. The idea would be not what a man could get from the State but what could he give to the State ... the war would ... destroy ... the inequality among the classes ... the brotherhood of man ... would be an established axiom of education.

He went on to say that education must be more practical and he wanted to see 'a much closer association between the state and great educational institutions'. The exclusion of women from active participation in 'the affairs of State' would be impossible after the 'magnificent service of womanhood' given in the war. He hoped fervently that

Manchester Grammar School, *c.*1918. (*Courtesy of Manchester Central Library Local Studies Collection*)

there would never be another war like it and 'he looked forward to a United States of Europe'.

However Miss S.A. Burstall, speaking of secondary education for girls, felt that the 'home side of girls' lives should be strengthened'. Girls should be taught more about the duty owed to family and it was through the family that they would best serve the State. 'Many women would have to do what was done in the Middle Ages; look after the family, the children, and carry on part of the industrial life of the nation as well.' She felt that the greatest needs in secondary education were preparatory schools for girls and more scholarships and fellowship, a need she felt was much greater in Manchester than in London. Professor J.J. Findlay felt that 'as a result of the war we are asking of everything', and that, although there was a certain idleness in the universities which need to be addressed, there was 'a danger of strain if the State determined to lay hold of youth for its own purposes ... and he feared the dead hand of the State over education'.

British newspapers printed encouraging reports of Allied advances and small victories on the Somme but the people of Manchester were not fooled. Everyone knew someone who had lost someone in the fighting. The numbers of wounded and their injuries told their own stories. One casualty in September which caused particular grief in Manchester was the death of a 'White Hope'. Harry Bilsbury was a boxer from Leigh. A tall strong sporting man, Harry was a good boxer and had taken part in the 'White Hope' competition at the Free Trade Hall in Manchester before the war. His 'hard hitting' was a noted feature, earning him the nickname of 'One Round', and he had also boxed in exhibitions at the Palace Theatre in the city. In addition he was a good fast runner and in that sport he was known as 'Long Span'. His death emphasized the potential of young life wasted as so many young lives were wasted. Conscription, however, remained compulsory.

There had also been pressure from women during the first two years of the war for their own uniformed service so that they could offer help with the war effort at the Front. Finally in December the Women's Auxiliary Army Corps (WAAC), later renamed Queen Mary's Army Auxiliary Corps, was established. A plea for conscription for women had failed but the suggestion that females be involved in front-line war work had now been accepted, although more out of necessity than choice. Women had proved themselves in so many spheres and the authorities realized that if they were sent to the Front to undertake non-combatant duties including cooking, cleaning, clerical work, driving, general maintenance work, ambulance duties or any other non-combatant chore, they could free up the men to fight. Things were getting desperate and this move was generally welcomed. Besides, there had long been horror stories of inept male cooks burning roasts and ruining food to the extent that the soldiers threw away what had been cooked rather than be forced to eat it.

The casualties from the Battle of the Somme were so high in July and August that even the Germans had become alarmed at the bloodshed and the toll on soldiers' lives. The Central Powers of Germany and Austria were also experiencing blockades and shortages of food and fuel in the same way as the Allies were suffering. In the early autumn the Germans put forward tentative peace proposals. The British government was unimpressed and the attempt was seen as part of a cunning plot by the Germans to trick the Allies into complacency. As Lloyd George drily remarked the Allies did not start the War and Britain was not the traitor in the Council of Europe. Only 'an unmistakable and unchallenged and complete' victory over the Germans was acceptable and Germany must be brought to heel, otherwise all the other sacrifices would have been made in vain. However, Lloyd George was also uncomfortably aware that this war wasn't just a war being fought on principle, it was a war being fought on the grounds of profits and principle in that order. More than one major business interest had told him 'Britain isn't yet ready to win the war'.

In Manchester this translated to the growing arms industry rather than the cotton trade for which the city was famous. Beyer Peacock led the way. The real heroes, or rather heroines, of the munitions industry were the women who worked in the munitions factories. Known initially as 'munitionettes' they were referred to affectionately as 'canaries' because of the yellow colour of their skin which was a result of exposure to TNT. Large numbers of female workers helped the war effort by making shells and fuses although it was dirty and often dangerous work. Incorrect or clumsy handling of components could result in lethal explosions. Many women suffered from health problems and a number also died through over-exposure to TNT. However, they also died quite young in the mills and at least the pay for making munitions was better, although still not equal to men's wages. But women were preferred for making munitions because

Women working in a Manchester munitions factory, *c.*1916. (*Courtesy of Manchester Central Library Local Studies Collection*)

their fingers were smaller and far more dextrous than those of men. By this time women were beginning to play a major role in other industries including making tyres, manufacturing sodium bicarbonate, glucose and glass sheets, making asbestos mattresses used to line the boilers of battleships, working in flour mills and also in oilseed mills producing food, soap and 'cakes' used for animal fodder, baking biscuits, mining coal and in transport facilities as well. Munitions, troops and supplies had to be moved from the city to the ports. Manchester had a ship canal linking the city to the port of Liverpool but it was on the wrong side of the country to efficiently service the needs of troops on the Continent.

Ports on the eastern seaboard were much better placed. In the city Victoria railway station was, and still is, the main station for trains to Yorkshire and Humberside and it was female workers who kept the trains running after many of the male staff had enlisted: 10,422 members of the Lancashire and Yorkshire Railway (27 per cent of the total staff) had enlisted in the armed forces and, of these, 1,465 were killed in action. Women became guards, porters, ticket collectors, office workers and ran the railway cafes. Females were not usually allowed to work in signal boxes being 'physiologically unsuited to the

Manchester Ship Canal, *c.*1910.

job', and they did not work as train drivers for the same reason that they did not work as tram drivers which was mostly a question of confidence, but there were also training issues and male prejudices to be overcome. A century on female drivers are still an object of derision to many male drivers despite their generally having much better safety records.

Following the introduction of conscription, a number of military tribunals were set up but the records of those in Manchester, like many in the rest of the country, were destroyed sometime in the 1920s. A tribunal usually consisted of about eight local dignitaries, sometimes fewer, and a couple of military men. Most hearings lasted about ten minutes. Any male who wished to be exempt from fighting had to appear before a tribunal. There were a number of reserved occupations which were considered essential for the war effort (farming, fishing, mining, manufacturing, shipbuilding etc), and there were those who had extensive family responsibilities, did voluntary work in hospitals or grew food on their allotments. Some were medically unfit, poor eyesight being one of the major reasons, plus a small number objected on religious or humanitarian grounds and it was these individuals who became known as conscientious objectors. Most who had such reservations were willing to carry out non-combatant roles such as medical orderlies or drivers or munitions work, but a few refused to make any contribution and were imprisoned. There were lengthy philosophical discussions on the principle of conscientious objectors. One school of thought believed that no one should be forced to fight for something in which he did not believe by a government for whom he could not vote. Another school of thought, endorsed by most serving soldiers, held that freedom of choice was important but some people had to fight and die for it because the Kaiser was not noted for either his democracy or his liberal attitudes. It was an impasse. A cruel side effect was that men not in khaki were generally viewed as cowards even though they might be working in a reserved occupation, be medically unfit or invalided out of the army, or simply on leave. The White Feather Brigade didn't see it that way. This organization, whose membership was mainly young attractive-looking girls, encouraged them to go up to any man not in uniform, be verbally offensive and present him with a white feather for cowardice. This practice eventually caused so much controversy and resentment that the Army issued khaki armlets for those on leave, those who had been assessed and couldn't serve, and those who were working in reserved occupations. Those who were genuine conscientious objectors got a rough ride. They would often be shunned by their family and friends, unable to find work since most employers flatly refused to employ conscientious objectors, and consequently they had no money to even feed themselves. A number lived rough in the countryside, stealing food from farms to survive. Manchester was fiercely proud of all its contributions to the war effort and, although the records are not extant, the city was not particularly tolerant of those who just refused to fight.

Toys had been imported from Japan and America in 1915 but then import tariffs imposed on toys and games in 1916 had virtually ended the trade. British toymakers generally suffered from an image of high prices (due to the rising prices of raw materials) and unreliable deliveries (due mainly to most available transport being commandeered for the war), but in the north-west the Primrose League (an organization founded in 1883 to promote the Conservative cause and free enterprise, which had taken Disraeli's favourite flower, the primrose, as its emblem) had been encouraging a fledgling cottage toy-making industry, although many workers in Manchester couldn't afford to buy toys for their children. It was conceded, however, that British toys, especially dolls and tin work, were generally inferior to

German ones. Christmas 1916 was a grim time for many in the city. The Battle of the Somme had officially ended on 18 November but casualties were still arriving in the city. Nurses did their best to decorate the hospital wards with holly and paper chains, and wounded soldiers in the various hospitals around the city had some of the best Christmas lunches of roast meats and plum puddings donated and prepared by grateful citizens who couldn't do enough for them. A contrast to the prison fare of conscientious objectors which was mainly rationed helpings of soup, potatoes, bread and rice. Those at the Front didn't always fare much better either. Christmas dinner for some of them was little more than jam or cheese on hard biscuits. Friends and family back home sent parcels of comforts but could only send non-perishable foods for the festive season. These, however, could and did include plum puddings and Christmas cake. Soldiers would share whatever they received with their comrades. They cheered themselves up by singing Christmas carols and trying to forget what lay on the other side of the trenches. One officer at the Front wrote in a letter home that Christmas 1916 was an awful winter. The cook and the rations lorry couldn't reach him and his comrades because of ice and snow on the roads. Christmas lunch for him was a tin of bully beef fried up over a small fire in a shallow ground trough. Back in Manchester there had been a number of Christmas appeals as usual and most children got a good square meal and perhaps an orange as a treat on Christmas Day, but for many folk a small tipple of rum or gin in the pub was all the Christmas good cheer they would see. Most people just desperately wanted to see the end of the war but as far as that was concerned they were simply crying for the moon.

CHAPTER 4

1917

Intercessionary services were held as usual in Manchester Cathedral and local churches on the first Sunday of the New Year but folk were finding it increasingly difficult to be cheerful and optimistic. The international situation and the German problem concerned them less than the deaths and injuries that their own loved ones were suffering. The war was taking a huge and deadly toll on husbands, sons, brothers and fathers fighting at the Front and after the catastrophe that was the Somme, stoicism was struggling with cynicism and despair. Added to that were the steadily rising prices and increasing shortages of essential foodstuffs and the scarcity of fuel. Meanwhile those in government circles, having promised a land fit for heroes to return to after the war, were wondering how on earth this was going to be achieved. Trade and capital and labour after the war were the subjects of much discussion and several conferences. Although big business interests were concerned, there was also a large degree of humanitarianism involved. The war was slowly breaking down class barriers. Large numbers of domestic staff had either enlisted or had left their employment to do war work which was more worthwhile and much better paid. The 'idle rich' world of hunting and shooting, sumptuous house parties and 'royal weekends' (when a member of the Royal Family would visit the home of some titled person) had all but disappeared. Twelve-course dinners, with luxury foods, the best china, solid silver cutlery and wine drunk out of delicate crystal glasses, all discreetly served under glittering chandeliers in large dining rooms where domestic staff were mostly viewed as 'nonpeople', were a thing of the past. The upper classes now fought side by side with the lower classes, suffering the same deprivations and hardships, each seeing the other as people for the first time rather than as lords and peasants. This was a dramatic change for most of those living in the city of Manchester because they, more than most, were painfully aware of the divide between the gilded lives of the mill-owners' families and those of ordinary workers living in dark, cramped and hopeless poverty. Less than fifty years before the start of the Great War, Britain had been severely criticized by her European neighbours for the treatment of her child workers, many of whom were little more than dispensable slaves. Cholera, typhoid and tuberculosis were regular occupational hazards among the backstreets of Manchester until it was finally realized that these diseases were no respecters of status, killing both rich and poor indiscriminately. Among women, debutantes had now begun working side by side with mill girls in the munitions factories, shops and offices, but mainly in the newly-formed Women's Land Army (see p. 52 below), each slowly gaining respect for the other. Now the talk about how the country should go forward after the war included seeing everyone as an individual with personal needs, and that there should be shorter working hours, decent meal breaks and better rates of pay. The need for a little leisure time for everyone was also recognized for the first time. 'There are idle lazy loafers in all ranks of society', wrote Sir W.H. Lever in the *Manchester Guardian*, but he believed that they were as much a product of 'the wrong conditions of life as ... consumption [tuberculosis]'. He also believed that 'two hours each day must be nationalised from the age of 14 to 18 for physical and mental education and from 18–22 for higher technical education'. They were fine words but reality still had a long way to go before his ideas could even be considered.

In May the Chancellor, Andrew Bonar Law, presented his war budget. To the surprise of many he did not add new levies. Interest rates on government repaid loans decreased from 5 per cent to 4.75 per cent, and he increased entertainment tax and tobacco duty and merged the munitions levy with excess profit duty, especially on shipping as he felt that the ship-owners were making too much of a profit. However, most ships were due to be requisitioned for war work and many ship-owners were left with the sense of a 'double whammy'. Freight charges had greatly increased and so too had the price of petrol, although it was felt that much petrol was being wasted on frivolous uses. What still really concerned most folk in Manchester though was the increase in profiteering and hoarding, which was having such a disastrous effect on food supplies as well as fuel and clothing, and there were protest meetings held in the city centre. Lloyd George, a staunch Liberal who had been born in Manchester's inner city suburb of Chorlton-on-Medlock, was furious that people

The Midland Hotel, Manchester, where Rolls-Royce had its beginnings, *c.*1912.

were deliberately withholding food and resources to force up prices which left the poorest without, and he vowed that he would break this heartless practice through food and fuel rationing despite all protests. To successfully fight the Germans he needed a country of effective, able-bodied citizens, not a bunch of half-starved runts, and he knew that underneath all the war effort and contribution that Manchester was making, the city was suffering badly at grass-roots level. The cotton industry was now in disarray. Hatting had been reduced to the making of Austrian-style felt hats, which although warm, were not the height of fashion or profitability. Coal mining was struggling owing to the numbers of miners who had enlisted. Engineering had been denuded of much of its skilled labour in the same way and so too had transport services for the same reason. In addition there was a threatened strike by railway engineers, drivers and firemen for the promise of an eight-hour day. It is not on record what those fighting at the Front thought when they read that piece of news in the *Manchester Guardian* although it is safe to say that they would not have been impressed.

At Manchester Victoria University, the distinguished New Zealand physicist Ernest Rutherford, who had won the Nobel prize for chemistry in 1908, had undertaken research which, in 1917, led to the splitting of the atom and the discovery of the proton. However, Manchester's major contributions on the home front during the Great War were the amounts of money, or 'silver bullets', the city donated to the war effort, engineering, munitions manufacture and hospitals. In December 1917 the city managed to achieve its target of raising enough money from businessmen and companies to pay for a tank. A real tank was sent for a week's display in Albert Square 'between the stone figures of John Bright and Bishop Fraser' to encourage donations and this, according to jealous neighbour Stockport, was the reason the target had been achieved. Stockport had received only a replica tank which had offended both the citizens and town council.

Manchester's chief engineering companies also played a vital part in the war effort. Mather & Platt, at their Park Works in Newton Heath, just outside the central city area, had acquiesced to the demands of the armed forces, and became a 'controlled establishment under the Munitions of War Act' in 1915. The company then turned out 'large quantities of shell casing and fuses were turned out and a howitzer re-lining department was established'. They had also supplied 'main propelling motors for submarines, gear boxes and hull

Tank 109 in a Manchester park. (*Courtesy of Manchester Central Library Local Studies Collection*)

plates for tanks, generators for searchlight duties and a multitude of other munitions of war'. Numbers of 'munitionettes' were employed and the fear was expressed that women were 'losing their femininity' by doing men's jobs, both in munitions and other spheres, becoming 'coarsened' as a result. As one writer put it 'Women do themselves know how their engagement in men's occupations is changing them ... changing their looks, their manner and their character ... women's very walk is becoming different ... you cannot ... be in a hurry without ... increasing the length of your stride ...' The Armstrong-Whitworth works in Openshaw manufactured guns, ammunition, ships and aircraft. A.V. Roe, established at Brownsfield Mill in Great Ancoats Street, pioneered the manufacture of light aircraft and the Avro 504 saw front-line service during the early part of the war and was then used as a training aircraft. There was, however, a lament that due to prejudice and sheer lack of forward thinking the training of female engineers had not begun soon after the war had started. 'If a little foresight had been exercised ... and girls of fifteen or sixteen had been apprenticed to the highly skilled sections of the engineering industry, a great number of men would have been liberated for the army ... instead we have thousands of young men ... in munitions works who cannot be spared.' It was also feared that women would be 'driven out of engineering after the war'. Although this did not happen completely, women were sufficiently discouraged so that even 100 years later engineering is still not seen as 'a female occupation'.

As a result of the Battle of the Somme the city's hospital resources had become even more severely stretched with the constant arrival of hospital trains full of often badly-injured men. Yet another hospital was now opened at Grangethorpe on the edge of the Platt Hall estate off Wilmslow Road. The house had belonged to Herbert Smith-Carrington, one of the directors of the Armstrong-Whitworth engineering company in Manchester. He died in March 1917 and the Red Cross bought the house, intending it for use as a convalescent home which could offer long-term nursing care to more seriously wounded servicemen. However, the Ministry of War was in urgent need of additional orthopaedic facilities because the orthopaedic hospital at the Ducie Avenue School hospital in nearby Whitworth Park was having difficulty coping with the influx of patients after the Battle of the Somme. Using War Office funding, the Red Cross agreed to build and equip six wards, an operating theatre, a gymnasium, an administrative block and nurses' accommodation in the grounds. Officers were cared for in the house itself and other ranks in the newly-built wards, patients being required to wear blue uniforms as a distinguishing mark. Local children were often sent to give cigarettes to the men in blue sitting on seats in the adjacent Platt Fields. Grangethorpe became a full military hospital and the centre for orthopaedic work in Manchester. A specialist medical team, notably including Professor Sir Harry Platt, was assembled and the hospital became noted for pioneer work in the reconstruction of damaged nerves in limbs, tendon transplants and bone grafts. Despite, it is said, using ordinary nails on occasion to pin bones together, it played a key role in devising and refining methods of treatment. Professor John Stopford, from the university's medical school (who went on to become the Vice-Chancellor of the University and for whom the current Medical School building is named) also worked at the hospital, treating 'gunshot wounds of peripheral nerves'. Grafton Elliott Smith, also from the university, worked with W.H.R. Rivers and T.H. Pear (Professor of Psychology at the university) on the nature and effect of shell shock. In total twenty-six members of the Medical School were directly involved in war work. Like Ashton General Hospital a few miles away, Grangethorpe Hospital also carried out pioneering with roentgen rays (more commonly known as X-rays), but at a price. Sergeant Jasper Redfern was in charge of the X-ray department but the dangers of exposure to radiation were not then fully understood

Grangethorpe Hospital, Manchester, *c.*1915. (*Courtesy of Manchester Central Library Local Studies Collection*)

and he gradually lost all his fingers as a result before dying of cancer in 1929. The *Manchester Guardian* paid tribute to the work done at Grangethorpe. 'At Grangethorpe you will find men who have brought the use of artificial limbs to so sensitive a pitch that with the touch of a wooden foot they will recognize such things as a small ball of paper, a pebble, a pencil, a cigarette ... men who walk so upright and alert that it would be a keen observer who recognized a wooden leg ... .men who run, jump over ... obstacles and kick footballs ...' To prove the point, the hospital even had a football team known as Grangethorpe Wanderers. The reputation of the hospital was such that both King George V and Field Marshal Haig paid a visit in the immediate aftermath of the war.

Withington Hospital, on Nell Lane in Didsbury, was just outside the main area of Manchester city centre. Originally a workhouse, it was converted into a hospital for poor people in 1864–6, with some assistance from the famous 'Lady with the Lamp', Florence Nightingale. In 1917 the hospital became virtually the only hospital camp in the country for German prisoners of war. Some local resentment was caused by the fact that the internees appeared to have larger food rations than English folk. For their part the Germans complained about the quality of English cooking and many began cooking for themselves. Strikes were becoming a serious problem by the start of 1917. Although many serving abroad still regarded strikes at home as a betrayal in wartime, those involved were struggling desperately to make ends meet as prices rose and the value of wages fell. In Manchester the cotton trade, and its 'spin-off sibling' the hatting trade, were in real trouble. Tariffs imposed on the cotton industry had put an end to the long-defended free trade but were a necessary measure to raise extra funds for the war. A heavy blow was that the Indian export trade had virtually ceased due to the country beginning to establish its own cotton-manufacturing industry, becoming overstocked with cotton cloth, and a bad monsoon season which lessened the demand for cotton goods. In 1915 cotton 'piece' exports to India were only 66 per cent of pre-war levels and continued to decline. Japan, less involved in the war, was also exporting cotton-manufacturing machinery and raw materials to India. In June 1916 the Manchester Chamber of Commerce noted considerable anxiety over the situation. By 1917 the problems of rising costs and increasing scarcity of available freight, the licensing of raw cotton imports, plus more competition in the market were taking their toll as well.

Raw materials were also in short supply as the government had not properly sought for alternative sources of supply (to America), there was a severe shortage of skilled workers, and wages were falling far behind rapidly-rising food and fuel prices and the annual increase in rents which continued despite the war and its hardships. Unfortunately in many cases there was simply no longer the money to pay the workers' demands. The first Russian Revolution, which had followed the assassination of Rasputin at the end of December 1916, was known as the February Revolution because Russia was still using the old Julian calendar. It actually occurred on 8 March in the Gregorian calendar which most of Europe used, and the support for the revolution in Britain was a shock to the authorities. A newspaper, published by Manchester suffragette Sylvia Pankhurst, was already in trouble for having celebrated the 1916 Easter Uprising in Dublin, and it now made the Russian revolution and the views of Lenin another cause for celebration. His slogan of 'Peace, Bread and Land' struck a chord with many workers, especially in the industrially-prosperous and socially-deprived north-west and particularly in the city of Manchester with its appalling slum conditions in which so many lived. Workers, who had been told for so long that they had nothing, they were nothing, and that they should be grateful for anything, began to see themselves in a whole new light. They did have something on which they could capitalise. They had their labour, and they watched events in Russia with fascination. From March to November 1917 there were a series of uprisings which eventually resulted in the abdication of the Tsar, Nicholas II, whom many Russians blamed for the monumental losses Russia was suffering in the Great War. In September Russia was declared a republic and there were strong indications that the country would withdraw from the war. King George V now faced a dilemma. Nicholas was his cousin, a man whom he liked very much, and, when he received a request for political asylum from the Russian imperial family, George's impulse, on a personal level, was to agree immediately. The government, seriously worried about the message that it would send to British workers, strongly advised him not to agree to Nicholas's request. After much soul-searching and struggles with his conscience, George eventually declined to give the Tsar and his family asylum. He knew it would mean inevitable death for his cousin but, constitutionally he felt he had little choice.

King George V and Queen Mary in Manchester, 14 July 1913.

George V was a man facing other problems as well, apart from the Tsar. The royal family were of exclusive German descent, and had been since the death of Queen Anne in 1714. The sole non-German member of the family was George's mother, Queen Alexandra, who was Danish. In addition he was facing the embarrassing prospect of ordering his subjects to fight another of his cousins, Kaiser Wilhelm, with whom he privately got on rather well. However, he knew that, after the tragedy of the Somme, anti-German feeling was running extremely high in Britain, and he felt that it was just too much to ask the British people to follow and fight for a King of German descent and bearing the very German name of Saxe-Coburg-Gotha. George V couldn't help his lineage but he could make a very public gesture of renouncing his German connections. After giving the matter a good deal of thought he issued a royal proclamation on 17 July 1917 which was read out on the steps of Manchester Town Hall. 'Now, therefore, We, out of Our Royal Will and Authority, do hereby declare and announce that as from the date of this Our Royal Proclamation, Our House and Family shall be styled and known as the House and Family of Windsor, and that all the descendants in the male line of Our said Grandmother, Queen Victoria, who are subjects of this realm ... shall bear the said Name of Windsor.' King George also knew that Lloyd George, Bonar Law, and most other MPs had given up their parliamentary salaries for the duration of the war as a personal contribution to the war effort. By now anxious to be seen doing his bit as well in making sacrifices, he insisted that the Royal Family lived on food rations and limited its members to two slices of bread per day. He also banned the use of alcohol in all royal residences. These gestures made him feel more at one with his subjects and many of them respected him for it. He had clearly demonstrated that his loyalties lay firmly with Britain.

In January 1917 the Women's Land Army (WLA) had been established under the leadership of Dame Meriel Talbot. In March the new organisation began recruiting women to work on the land. Village registrars were appointed to keep registers of local women farm workers so that farmers knew who was available in their areas and the particular skills of each woman. A women's war agricultural committee was set up to look after the women's interests and to persuade farmers to take on female staff. Each woman who joined the Land Army was given a uniform which consisted of breeches, tunic, boots, leggings, a mackintosh, jersey and soft felt hat. That the uniform included breeches initially sent frissons of shock and horror through the male members of society although they were mainly accepted cheerfully enough by those who wore them. They gave much more freedom of movement than long skirts and were much more practical. However, the handbook for WLA members cautioned that 'you are doing a man's work and so you're dressed rather like a man, but

Women's Land Army personnel in Manchester, c.1917. (*Courtesy of Manchester Central Library Local Studies Collection*)

remember just because you wear a smock and breeches you should take care to behave like a British girl who expects chivalry and respect from everyone she meets'. Several WLA members also had their hair cut short into a more manageable bob, which caused further consternation. Nevertheless, on health and safety grounds, it was a sensible move. Suitable accommodation was found for women who were to live away from home and there were further misgivings voiced about allowing women so much freedom and independence. WLA training centres and existing agricultural colleges provided short, intensive training courses of up to three months for females learning to work on the land. Once employed on the land the women were to be paid a decent living wage, if rather less than male labourers.

For girls in Manchester the WLA also provided a means of escape from the mills, manufactories and heavy smogs of the city into open countryside and fresh air and there were many enthusiastic volunteers. Initially there was fierce resistance to female farm workers, but the government continued to stand firm and refused to repatriate soldiers serving at the front for sowing and harvesting crops. A trained army of women was available for the work and if they were not hired then the farmers would be the losers. Finally forced to accept the idea of female labour, some farmers took the plunge and were amazed to find how adaptable and efficient their female workers were. Word spread quickly and WLA members were soon working very successfully on farms around the country. A women's forestry corps was also established to manage trees and woodlands. Wood was important in shipbuilding, construction and even as fuel.

The food situation was continuing to give grave cause for concern. There was a severe shortage of wheat and, as a result, 'government bread' was introduced in March. The flour for this bread was a mixture of oats, barley, rye and some potato flour, giving the bread a dark colour which made it unpopular despite its nutritional value. Apart from porridge, bread with margarine and jam or dripping (juices dripped from meat, usually beef) was the staple diet of many working-class children. Tea, sugar, bacon, butter and meat were also suffering shortages. German U-boats had been blockading British merchant shipping since the autumn of 1914 and had sunk a large amount of tonnage in an attempt to starve Britain into submission. The Germans now decided to declare submarine warfare on every commercial ship bound for Britain. This included numbers of American ships, which enraged the United States and in April America declared war on the

Central Powers and joined the Allies. However, imports dwindled and British farmers were struggling to keep up a sufficient supply. The situation was made worse through hoarding and profiteering. Those who were better off bought more meat or bacon than they needed and they would also buy the cheaper cuts which meant that poorer folk got little or nothing at all. In an attempt to resolve this situation National Kitchens were introduced in May. The idea was that, as it was cheaper to buy in bulk which would be more affordable with national funding, the kitchens could produce thousands of hot, cheap, nutritious meals each day which would especially benefit poorer folk. Initially this had the unfortunate result of giving the project a soup-kitchen image and people's pride was offended since they believed that if they frequented these kitchens they would be seen as poor charity cases. The first kitchens were very functional, often with nowhere to sit down, and not especially welcoming. An image overhaul was ordered to make the kitchens into pleasant cafes for ordinary people and this greatly increased their appeal. A two-course meal was available for 6d which consisted of soup, meat and two vegetables or a main course and a pudding. The kitchens were sometimes staffed by volunteers, often upper middle-class women keen to help with the war effort, but mostly the cooks, servers and cashiers were paid. There were several such National Kitchens in the city of Manchester, the largest of which served up 3,000 meals a day. Despite everything however food shortages continued and were slowly becoming worse. Hotels and restaurants were ordered to have meatless days on Wednesdays and Fridays, although as fish was not included, they could serve fish dishes for a main course on the days meat was not available. The size of bread was regulated and loaves could only be of four types and had to weigh either 1lb (0.5kg) or an even number of pounds. Cakes and biscuits requiring wheat flour, and quantities of fruit, sugar and butter were virtually banned, especially as eggs were also scarce. In the *Manchester Guardian* it was reported that there were calls by Captain Bathurst (Parliamentary Secretary to the Food Controller) speaking at a conference in Oxford, for stricter economy and criticism of 'eating-house guzzling', plus complaints about hoarding by the better-off folk and the food consumed by racehorses and dogs. The country had just a month's supply of potatoes left, he said, and the current wheat supplies had to last for at least a further five months. He proposed that potatoes should be left for the poor and the habit of 'teas' (parish teas, school teas, afternoon teas) should be abolished. A cake and pastry order was being passed to ensure a severe reduction in the manufacture of these sweet treats to force the public to cut down on flour, sugar and such eating habits. Consumption of bread also needed to be cut by one-third and this should be done by classes who did not depend on bread for their staple food. He maintained that toast was the most un-economical way of eating bread. There was a world shortage of wheat and the failure of the potato harvest in 1916 due to potato blight had not helped the situation. The Germans might have succeeded in cur-tailing the supply of foodstuffs with their constant attacks on British merchant shipping but they were not going to starve the country into submission. Dogs would not be ordered to be destroyed but they were not to be fed on dog biscuits or other grain products. However, the oat rations for a single racehorse could support up to thirty people and the wisdom of continuing racing as a sport had to be questioned urgently. If Captain Bathurst had hoped that his appeals would be heeded, he was in for a disappointment. Nationally they fell on deaf ears. The mass of poor folk in Manchester depended on bread and potatoes as the main staples of their diet and those Mancunians who could afford to do so were generally not minded to alter either their shopping or their eating habits. By the early autumn it had become painfully obvious that some food rationing was inevitable.

Juvenile crime had become an increasing problem in towns and cities throughout the war. In 1917 H.M. Chief Inspector of Reforma-tory and Industrial Schools, Charles Russell, had published a paper on 'The Problem of Juvenile Crime' and singled out Manchester for special attention. Adult crime had decreased all over the country, no doubt due to the fact, Russell believed, that so many actual or potential perpetrators of it were serving in the armed forces. The 'crimes' were mostly vandalism or petty theft, the result of 'increased opportunities for misapplied energy'. Russell had no doubt that 'at the back of all the trouble lies the national disgrace of the slum'. He also criticised the use of the excuse that it was 'the influence of the cinema' which was responsible, considering that to be a red herring, although admitting that 'the present film stories are penny-dreadfuls in action'. However, he did state that 'in most of the pictures seen, their vulgarity and silliness and the distorted unreal Americanised (in the worst sense) view of life presented must have a deteriorating effect …' and, Russell believed, this encouraged 'thoughts of burglary'. He added that in Manchester a gang of six boys stole sweets and cigarettes, dividing up their spoils at the house of one whose father was in the Army and whose mother was out at work. The most successful thief among them was awarded a ribbon to wear in his buttonhole. Despite the usual excuses of absentee fathers and working mothers, Russell felt that a lack of discipline and attention by the parents was more likely to be responsible than their actual physical whereabouts. He quoted Spurley Hey's enquiry into the records of the Manchester Juvenile Court which showed that boys alone were responsible for the increase in juvenile crime and that the general number of offences by girls had decreased. During 1915 the number of offences by boys in the city had risen to 781, an increase of 62 per cent on the previous year, and convictions rose from 154 to 209. The greatest increase appeared to be among boys aged 11–12, although Russell acknowledged that there were similar problems before the war. He lamented the general state of education and insisted that in order to check boyish delinquency it was absolutely essential that healthy physical exercise and games were provided for boys and that they should join some sort of club once they reached the age of 12. Russell finally concluded, however, that 'the responsibility for all crime lies with inequality and injustice of our social system'.

In the summer of 1917 the Government finally acknowledged what many had long realized, that a great debt of gratitude was owed to all the women of England for 'keeping the home fires burning', doing many of the jobs previously done by men, caring for the sick and wounded, sending food parcels and 'comforts' to soldiers, and so much more besides, while the men were away fighting. In fact the Chief Inspector of Factories and Workshops in 1916 admitted that there was a '... great adaptability of women in substitution ...'. Female suffrage had received large measures of support from various Liberal Party factions and the fledgling Labour Party (born in 1906 from Keir Hardie's Independent Labour Party) which had found much support in the northern mill towns. In March 1917 the Manchester and District Federation of Women's Suffrage Societies organized a 'memorial'. This took the form of a letter, signed by 4,000 'influential persons' from the city of Manchester and its constituencies mainly in what is now known as Greater Manchester together with a couple from Cheshire and High Peak in Derbyshire. It stated that, following the government conference on electoral reform, 'We, the undersigned, urge the necessity of enfranchising women in any proposed electoral reform brought forward during the war, so that they shall take part in the election of the parliament which will deal with the problems of reconstruction immediately after the war.' The government agreed and finally the proposed changes to the Electoral Reform Bill became law. Women over the age of 30 were given the vote. The property qualification (i.e. needing to be a property owner in order to vote) was also abolished. Thousands of women in Manchester were jubilant, and so were their sisters in other towns and cities throughout Britain. Amazingly, some of the remaining opponents of female suffrage, especially in the north of England, were women themselves, who felt 'that sort of thing was best left to the men', and until the 1970s it was common for women to vote the same way as their husbands because they either wanted to do so or were told to do so. However, it was a good start for the liberation of women, although they still did not have equal rights in many spheres and universal suffrage (the right to vote for everyone) would not become law until 1928. Proxy voting for absentee residents, prompted by the large number of troops serving overseas, was also introduced. The former six single-member parliamentary constituencies of Manchester East, Manchester North, Manchester North East and Manchester North West, Manchester South and Manchester South West were abolished under the electoral boundary redistribution in 1918 and the city of Manchester would have its representation increased to ten MPs. Today (2016) there are four main Manchester city constituencies: Manchester, Central; Manchester, Blackley (to the north); Manchester, Gorton (to the east); and Manchester, Withington (to the south).

The Government finally agreed in late summer that there should be a sugar permit scheme. Shoppers would have to get a form from the Post Office, register and when they received their card, deposit it with a designated shopkeeper of their choice and collect their rations on a weekly basis. Some 8 million cards were issued until the Government realized that the total number of applications for sugar cards exceeded the total population by several million and withdrew the scheme. There were growing concerns too over gross inequalities in food distribution and it was announced that in the New Year food cards would be distributed on which weekly supplies of sugar, tea, butter, bacon, margarine, flour, jam, syrup, tinned milk and matches would be marked for each person. Supplies would be distributed to the shopkeepers in proportion to the number of customers they had

Market Street junction with Cross Street, Manchester, c.1914. (*Courtesy of Manchester Central Library Local Studies Collection*)

and each shopkeeper was required to divide all weekly supplies proportionately among those registered. Initially tea, margarine, butter, bacon, and meat would be rationed in addition to sugar which had been rationed for some time. A list of weekly food rations for adults was published which stipulated that every adult should receive 5lbs (2.5kg) of potatoes; 1lb (0.5kg) each of carrots, onions and rice; 2lbs (1kg) of green vegetables; 1lb (0.5kg) of fresh fruit; and 2lbs (1kg) of meat as well as four eggs, one large loaf and four pints (two litres) of milk at fixed prices each week. It was the sort of diet that the poor in the slums of Manchester had only ever dreamed about. Nevertheless, it would mean everyone got at least some bread, potatoes, meat, fresh fruit and vegetables regularly.

Fuel was to be rationed as well. There had already been some rationing the previous autumn but now this was to be increased because there was a very serious shortage of coal. Although the output of the mines had declined dramatically due to miners enlisting in the armed services, much of the available coal was needed for both transport and for those at the Front. Regular railway services had dramatically declined. There were no cheap excursion trains at holiday periods and trains were often cancelled during festive periods to discourage the general population from attempting to travel. Most trains which did run were either troop trains or cargo trains for it was essential that men and supplies could be transported as necessary.

The advertisements in the *Manchester Evening News* for 1917 gave a glimpse of life in the city at that time. Unlike newspapers in the neighbouring town of Stockport, which advertised furs and evening dresses and luxury goods alongside the more mundane items, the *Manchester Evening News* advertisements concentrated on food, health remedies and some cigarettes. Cigarette packets then did not carry a government health warning and smoking was seen as a pleasure acceptable everywhere. Player's Navy Cut cigarettes were a very popular brand which were supplied duty-free to wounded soldiers and sailors. Brito margarine lashed out at profiteers, trumpeting that Brito's profit margins were fixed and, as a large turnover had decreased the costs of production per item, their customers were benefitting from the resulting price reduction. Veda Bakeries in Hulme boasted that their bread 'remained soft, fresh and sweet' in factory conditions and claimed that this was the ideal bread for war workers. Liver salts and tonic wines were promoted as the remedy for a whole range of ailments from flu, fatigue and brain fog to insomnia, indigestion, neuralgia, hysteria and headache. One such remedy, Andrews' Liver Salts, is still available today.

A poster was published at Christmastime 1917 summing up the food situation for the whole country. It showed a woman holding an empty frying pan and read 'No butter, no lard, no treacle, no eggs, no sugar, no tea, no bacon, no beef, no beer, no anything! Looks jolly for Christmas, don't it?' While that wasn't quite the whole truth, it summed up the general cynical feelings of the population towards the continuing harsh austerity forced on the country by the conditions of war. There were restrictions on the amount of fruit, fat, sugar and flour that could be used in Christmas puddings and cakes, and for many in Manchester boiled brisket or a boiled chicken replaced the more traditional roast goose, beef or pork for Christmas lunch. The newspaper magnate Lord Northcliffe offered advice on what gifts to send in Christmas parcels to men serving at the Front. These included

6th Battalion, Manchester Regiment, August 1914. (*Courtesy of Manchester Central Library Local Studies Collection*)

'soup, toothbrushes, writing paper and envelopes ... the best sweets are chewing gum, chocolate and bullseyes ... the bullseyes ought to have plenty of peppermint in them for it keeps those who suck them warm on a cold night'. The *Manchester Guardian* had organized a Christmas fund from its offices in Cross Street for money or items for parcels which could be sent to those at the Front. The list of items requested far exceeded the recommendations of Lord Northcliffe and included 'cigarettes, tobacco, matches, candles, comforts. Balaclava hats, mackintoshes, handkerchiefs, soap, razors, toothpaste, boot polish, needles and cotton, anti-frostbite grease, insect powder, cutlery, sweets, tinned foods, writing implements, records, footballs, books and magazines' to name but a few. Many of the items might have been expected to be issued as part of the soldiers' kit but there was considerable disorganization and lack of funds at the War Office and it was left to the already hard-pressed public to supply such things to their own nearest and dearest. There were also a large number of patriotic postcards and Christmas cards on sale but folk preferred to spend what money they had on practical gifts or 'comforts' rather than cards and, while the number of parcels sent increased, the number of cards decreased. A big effort was made to give wounded soldiers in the hospitals a decent Christmas dinner and carol concerts or other entertainments were organized for them, but the general mood of Christmas 1917 in the city however was sombre, depressed and despairing of the war ever ending. Then, on the last day of the year, sugar ration cards were issued in Manchester. Official rationing of food had begun.

CHAPTER 5

1918

The usual intercessionary services were held on the first Sunday of the year but folk in Manchester, like folk elsewhere, had little heart for them. They attended out of duty and perhaps a faint hope that 1918 might actually be the last year of the war. Many wondered exactly how long things could go on as they were. In April the Military Conscription Act extended the age for conscription up to fifty for men and no-one quite knew where it was all going to end. A note of desperation was beginning to creep in. Women did not just serve as part of the Army. Towards the end of 1917 the Women's Royal Naval Service had been established, to be followed by the Women's Royal Air Force in April 1918. The women would be given a uniform, accommodation, a ration card and a wage. For women and girls from the Manchester millscapes it was not only a chance to 'do their bit', it was a chance to escape the dank poverty of their lives, to have a comparatively decent standard of living doing something useful and constructive', even perhaps a bit of real excitement. Horror was expressed in several quarters that women might be trained to kill out of necessity, that this was all totally wrong, but recruiting had become a numbers game and over 100,000 women had served at the Front by the end of the war.

Back in 1909 the Committee of Imperial Defence had declared that aircraft 'had no foreseeable military purpose'. Although Manchester had an airfield during the Great War at Trafford Park (in what is now the Greater Manchester area) its use was sporadic at best and it closed in 1918. Aircraft were still in their infancy and flying limits could be quite low. Towns and cities nearer to the east coast were better placed for aerial attack, and by the end of the war 4,000 aircraft and pilots had logged in total several thousand flying hours nationally. However, it was in the field of aeronautical engineering that Manchester played its part. In May 1918 the Alexandra Park Aerodrome, which was close to the city centre, was opened by the

War Department for the assembly, test flying and delivery of planes for the newly-formed Royal Air Force (RAF). The RAF was the result of a merger between the Army's Royal Flying Corps and the Royal Naval Air Service. The planes were manufactured by A.V. Roe (AVRO) at Newton Heath, a Manchester suburb, and at the National Aircraft Factory No. 2 at Heaton Chapel, then on the Manchester-Cheshire boundary. The planes were brought to the aerodrome in pieces, mostly by rail. Alexandra Park, just to the south of the city centre, had its own railway station. The war ended about six months later but the airfield saw AVRO operate the first scheduled domestic passenger air service in Britain. The 45-minute flight operated once a day leaving from Alexandra Park at 2.00pm and flying via Southport to Blackpool, arriving in Blackpool at 2.45pm. AVRO 504 three-seater biplanes were mostly used and a return ticket cost 9 guineas (just over £400 today).

On the streets of central Manchester in January 1918, however, the talk was all of the new rationing scheme coming into operation. Food ration cards would be distributed on which weekly supplies of sugar, tea, butter, bacon, flour, jam, syrup, tinned milk and matches would be marked for each person. First, everyone had to register with one shop to purchase these foodstuffs and, once registered, could not go elsewhere for them. No shopkeeper was required to register more customers than they could properly handle. Supplies would be distributed to the shopkeepers in proportion to the number of customers they had. Each shopkeeper was required to divide all weekly supplies proportionately among those registered. Initially margarine, butter, bacon and meat would be rationed in addition to sugar which had been rationed since the end of the previous year. However, there were some delays in issuing the food coupons and organizing equitable distribution, which was irritating to everyone, and there were still queues for margarine and milk. In mid-February Lord Rhondda also ordered a voluntary surrender of hoarded food, but this met with limited success, as was only to be expected. Poorer folk could not understand the desire to hoard, thus forcing others to make do with the left-overs or scraps. Many were used to sharing what little they had just to survive. Among the hoarders, however, there was a school of thought which insisted that if one person didn't hoard then another person would do so and, given that situation, why shouldn't folk hoard if they could afford to do so. It was their duty to feed their families as well as they could. Another kind of survival instinct kicking in.

On 6 February the *Manchester Evening News* published the following item on food hoarding:

By order of the Food Controller, from Monday next until the following Monday, food hoarders will be allowed to unburden themselves of their surplus food supplies through the local food committees, and will be paid half the price of the food of which they are dispossessed. After the lapse of the period of grace ... all tolerance of food hoarding will be at an end. Imprisonment will be the fate of everyone and anyone who is found guilty of the shabby practice of accumulating large stores of surplus necessaries at a time when everyone should be on short commons and exercising his bit of self-denial ... the ordinary householder is already bound by the regulation that 'no person shall after April 9th 1917, acquire any article of food so that the quantity of the article in his possession or under his control at any time exceeds the quantity required for ordinary use in his household or establishment ...' although there are some who say they ought not to be interfered with although they have accumulated six month's supply ...

In the first two years of the war food prices rose by 61 per cent. By 1918 they had almost doubled. Therefore it was not just the rationed quantity of foods allowed which needed to be stable: the prices also needed to be fixed, or at least limited. Wheat and milk were the first commodities, followed by bacon and meat. Allotment holders and smallholders, as well as individuals around the country who had their own gardens, were growing as much produce as they could. Flower-beds were dug over and potatoes planted. Local provincial papers gave hints and tips on what to plant and when to plant it and how to nurture it. Parks and public spaces were taken over for growing crops. This did not really affect the city centre area of Manchester since every square inch was covered with mills, warehouses, business premises, manufactories and numerous streets of terraced workers housing. Determined however that everyone would have a fair share of the food available a list of weekly food rations was published by the government:

- 2oz tea [approx. sixteen tea bags or 65g]
- 8oz sugar [250g]
- 4 pints milk [2 litres]

- 1 loaf [large brown; 2lbs/1kg in weight which is that of an average large uncut loaf]
- 4oz butter [125g]
- 4oz margarine [125g]
- 4oz cheese [125g] Cheddar or Cheshire or Lancashire
- 4 eggs
- 2oz bacon [65g – works out at two rashers]
- 2lb meat [1kg – stewing steak, mince beef, lamb, mutton, liver, kidneys, rabbit, cow's heel]
- 1lb porridge oats [500g]
- 5lbs potatoes [2.5kg]
- 1lb carrots [500g]
- 1lb onions [500g]
- 2lbs [1kg] green vegetables [cabbage, kale, sprouts, in winter; + peas, beans, etc in summer]
- 1lb [500g] fruit [apples/pears in winter = two small apples + two small pears; + berries in summer]
- ½lb [250g] rice
- 1 small jar of preserves [marmalade, damson or summer fruit jam, apple or redcurrant jelly]

There were various grumbles such as there not being enough bread and the amount of butter, margarine and bacon were considered low, but there were few complaints about the quality of the food allowed, just the quantity. Almost a hundred years later, in January 2015, two healthy adults volunteered to live for a week on nothing but the rations stated in the list. At the end of the week their verdict was that they felt amazingly well but rather peckish. Exactly the same as folk said in 1918. During the months following the introduction of food rationing, the overall effect on the population was amazing and for the poor in the slums of Manchester the revelation was dramatic. The common diseases of malnutrition, such as rickets (lack of calcium), scurvy (lack of Vitamin C), anaemia (lack of iron), vitamin deficiencies, and stunted growth, were completely eradicated for the first time. Coal rationing was also in force and there were plans for further economies in the use of electric lighting and gas. Coal now cost 2s 6d per ton with an extra 10d for bagging. Sometimes it seemed that almost everything in life had been rationed. However, in late July there was a glut of herrings so fifteen barrels of the fish were distributed among the Red Cross hospitals of the Manchester area. At the same time Manchester council and several other local organizations continued to organize free classes in baby care, child welfare and basic cookery. Infant mortality in Manchester during the war was around 129/1,000 although it had fallen to under 109/1,000 by the end. The harsh realization that a whole generation had been lost, and needed to be replaced, focussed on the birth, successful nurturing and education of what was seen as the replacement generation.

Since the beginning of the twentieth century successive governments had been introducing legislation aimed at improving provision for children's education and welfare, raising the school leaving age, offering a wide choice of different schools, providing school meals, and, latterly, arranging facilities for children in the school holidays. There were now large numbers of absentee fathers and working mothers, especially in northern industrial cities like Manchester, which urgently raised the whole question of child care for younger children under the age of five. It had become the practice for harassed mothers to 'quieten' their children with 'soothing syrups'. There were a number on the market with names including the words elixir, cordial, draught or syrup. Godfreys Cordial had long been one of the most well-known; so too were Dalby's Carminative, Daffy's Elixir and Street's Infant Quietness. There were regional favourites and in Manchester Slowe's Infant Preservative was the most popular. Unfortunately the basis of these concoctions were laudanum or opium. Opiates had been in widespread use throughout the nineteenth century, a social problem highlighted by Arthur Conan Doyle in his Sherlock Holmes stories, and there had long been campaigns against their use. Thomas de Quincy, in his *Confessions*, although an opium user himself, exposed the problem in Manchester. He wrote '... some years ago, on passing through Manchester, I was informed by several cotton manufacturers, that their work people were rapidly getting into the practice of opium eating; so much so, that on a Saturday afternoon the counters of the druggists were strewed with pills of one, two or three grains, in preparation for the known demand of the evening. The immediate occasion of this practice was the lowness of wages, which, at that time, would not allow them to indulge in ale or spirits ...'. De Quincy was writing in the nineteenth century and, for adults, alcohol had largely replaced opium as a means of escape, although those who could afford it still used opium. Opium, however, could not solve the problem of daily child care. There were a few 'kindergartens' but these did not really cater for the development of children because often the expectation was that the children should remain indoors, quietly sitting still. Mindful of the urgent task of replacing the 'lost generation' with a new, intelligent and healthy generation, lateral thinking was applied to the problem and the idea of nursery education for children aged 2 to 5 was born. The 1918 Education Act, more commonly known as the Fisher Act after its instigator, was passed in August 1918 just four years after the start of the war. It charged local education authorities (LEAs) with attending to the 'health and physical condition of the children' as well as to their educational needs. It also required them to provide holiday camps, medical inspections, resources for children with special needs and free nursery schools for children aged 2 to 5. Manchester was one of the first cities in the country, along with London, Edinburgh and Birmingham, to offer free nursery education for its infants.

On 21 March the 16th Battalion Manchester Regiment had been given the task of defending Manchester Hill, which overlooked the town of St Quentin, from the German army which was reinforcing its positions on the Western Front. Manchester Hill was so named after its capture by the 2nd Battalion Manchester Regiment in 1917. The commanding officer of the 16th Battalion was Lieutenant Colonel Wilfrith Elstob, whose parents lived in Cheshire. Things went badly wrong when the Germans attacked under cover of early morning fog which rendered signalling devices and machine-gun defences useless. Heavy fighting continued all day and the Manchesters suffered heavy losses before being forced to surrender. Of the eight officers and 160 men who went into battle on Manchester Hill only two officers and fifteen men survived. However, the defence of Manchester Hill delayed the German advance, which had been the intention, and Lieutenant Colonel Elstob, who had fought valiantly despite being wounded three times, was awarded a posthumous Victoria Cross. The city of Manchester went into collective mourning but grieving proudly for the achievement of its battalion, and on 15 April a memorial service was held in Manchester Cathedral to honour the dead soldiers. It must have seemed a kind of divine retribution and sign of approval when, six days later, Germany's 'Red Baron', Manfred von Richthofen, was finally shot down and killed, either by a Canadian pilot, Captain Arthur Roy Brown, or by Australian army machine gunners on the ground. The 'Red Baron' (so called because of his title and the fact that he had his aeroplane painted red) was responsible for shooting down eighty Allied aircraft and he seemed invincible in the skies. His name and his actions passed into legend and the chorus of an American pop song commemorating him in the mid-1960s ran:

Ten, twenty, thirty, forty, fifty or more
The bloody Red Baron rolled up the score
Eighty men died trying to end that spree
Of the bloody Red Baron of Germany.

In late May the Americans joined in the action on the Western Front and, for the Germans, it was the beginning of the end. The final German offensive took place around Reims on 15 July, the Germans being routed on 17 July. On the same day the Russian Imperial Family were executed at Yekaterinburg. On 8 August the Allies began the 100 days' offensive, the final offensive of the Great War, and on 27 September they broke through the Hindenburg Line, the last line of the German defences in France. The end of the war was finally in sight but by then the citizens of Manchester had to suffer something far more local and sinister and heart-breaking.

In the early summer a type of flu virus had made its appearance in the north-west. At first the medical authorities were not unduly worried but it spread quickly and rapidly attained epidemic proportions. The British press was still under censorship in July 1918 and did not report the flu epidemic but Spain, neutral in the Great War, still had a free press, and reported on what soon became a pandemic as the virus spread around the world. For this reason the flu was nicknamed the 'Spanish Lady' or 'Spanish flu' although the first recorded case was actually in America at Camp Fuston in Kansas. However further research shows three waves. The first wave was in hospital camps in northern France during the winter of 1917. The second wave, September–December 1918, and the third wave, February–April 1919, were the lethal ones which caused so many deaths. Altogether 100 million people died: 40 million in India, 2.5 per cent of the populations in France, Germany and America, and at least 250,000 in Britain. It is said to have killed more people globally than the feared Black Death (bubonic plague). The disease, a particularly vicious type of avian flu, caused widespread disruption and virulently attacked the 20 to 40 age group, already depleted by the war. Cause of death was usually fluid flooding the lungs. Although the war wasn't responsible for the actual virus, it was responsible for its rapid spread through exhausted and vulnerable populations. During the week in which the Armistice was signed, flu killed 150 people in Manchester. One of the saddest accounts comes from a 7-year-old girl who lived in Greenheys, an area bordered by Moss Side, Hulme and Chorlton-on-Medlock close to Manchester city centre. The 'Spanish Lady' killed her mother, her father and a younger brother. She herself also suffered the virus but survived. The main symptom she remembers is a crippling headache. She also remembers the funerals of her parents and her little brother. Her father's coffin, draped with the Union Jack, as he was a member of the Royal Army Medical Corps, lay on a gun carriage, and her mother's coffin lay in a hearse with her 4-year-old brother's coffin tucked under the driver's seat. Black horses with plumes made of ostrich feathers pulled the coffins to Manchester's southern cemetery. She considered herself lucky that her grandmother took her in with her surviving siblings and brought them all up together. Many children orphaned in this way ended up in the workhouse, a cold, comfortless and loveless place where children had to work hard for their basic keep.

There were intercessionary services in Manchester to mark the fourth anniversary of the war and for the first time in four years the congregation had a glimmer of hope that the end of this dreadful war really was in sight. Lloyd George meanwhile was contemplating a general election that autumn. However, the new registers, including women voters and previously disenfranchised male voters, plus the re-aligning of parliamentary constituency boundaries, was taking

Freedom of the City of Manchester granted to David Lloyd George in 1918. (*Courtesy of Manchester Central Library Local Studies Collection*)

some time, although Bonar Law promised to have them ready for the end of October. Lloyd George, who had originally planned for the elections to be held in November, put back the date to mid-December. He realized that domestic issues such as childcare, female employment, education and rights, would need to be addressed to attract the female voters. In the meantime the former Liberal Prime Minister H.H. Asquith paid a visit to the city of Manchester to give an election address on behalf of the Liberals. He praised both the Army and the Navy and he paid tribute to the British troops. He wanted a 'clean peace and the setting up of an international polity which will chain up forever the furies of war'. Asquith defined a 'clean peace' as a 'peace which attains for the world the objects for which we have been fighting which is clean in the sense that it cleans the slate, but clean also in a higher sense that (as was wisely said here in Manchester the other day) it does not offend the conscience of either victor or mankind. You can have no clean peace if you have a continuance of veiled war ... a peace which is designed to inflict permanent humiliation ... to dismember what is by nature and affinity united, to leave open wounds ...' He went on to cover events and the current situation in Austria, Belgium, Russia, and Germany. International polity was to be in the form of a League of Nations whose remit would be to abolish war as a means of settling disputes. It would need to have the resources for intervention, conciliation and judicial arbitration. Any decisions or action could only be undertaken 'through common will'. He added that 'war under modern conditions has become a form of insanity and suicide ... the next great war will bring about the practical extinction of civilisation and the permanent crippling of the human race'.

Asquith finally turned his attention to the forthcoming general election and, although he paid tribute to the Coalition, he doubted the wisdom of holding an election at that point in time due to the imminent ending of the war. Mindful of the change in national and international affairs and the rise of the new young Labour Party, he put forward a case for the old values of true Liberalism before moving on to post-war policy. There was the matter of the Irish problem which required careful and delicate handling. A more immediate problem would be suitable provision for the returning soldiers and sailors which would fall into three main categories. Employment for able-bodied men. Assistance and training for those who could no longer do their former jobs. Adequate pensions enabling those who

King George V and Queen Mary at the Town Hall, Manchester in 1915. (*Courtesy of Manchester Central Library Local Studies Collection*)

were disabled to live in comfort. There had been disquiet through-out the war about lack of opportunities and inadequate pensions for those discharged from the armed forces. He made a strong case for the ending of censorship and a return to free speech as soon as the war had ended, as well as 'the subordination of special interests and the privileges of particular classes for the general good ...'. Asquith also spoke passionately about the benefits of free trade, especially to the British economy, and felt that it was unthinkable to retain tariffs after the war had ended. British prosperity depended on free trade. He also believed that fiscal arrangements should not be forced on the Dominions either; but he ruled out using economic boycotts after the war, seeing them as 'inconsistent with a clean peace'. The war debt was a serious economic problem: £8,000,000,000, (£351,500,000,000) had been spent to date supporting the war, plus interest, and then there would be the question of reconstruction after the war, including pensions, education, health and housing. There were, said Asquith, only two ways of meeting it, either through 'increased efficiency of capital and labour' or through taxation. The demolition of urban and rural slums was urgent and 400,000 new houses would be needed, and that was only the start. Added to this was the health and education of the young, the well-being of the elderly, shorter working hours, proper holiday leave, and a system of superannuation. Asquith foresaw what he termed 'a national minimum' in which 'every British citizen, man, woman or child, has in possession or within reach a standard of existence, physical, intellectual, moral, social, which makes life worth living, and ... does not block, but opens the road to its best and highest possibilities'. It was a powerful address but history defeated his good intentions.

Peace notes had been exchanged between President Wilson of the United States and Germany since October but there had been some who had questioned the gesture. Are we ready for peace, they asked. There was a diversity of views on a peace settlement and the 'enormity of the post war social reconstruction work'. Lloyd George had not been too far wide of the mark when he said that the Great War had been fought on grounds of business as much as anything else. However, on one issue everyone seemed to be united – The Kaiser had to go. German alliances were beginning to crumble. In mid-October the Germans suspended their submarine warfare. On 29 October the Croatians, Serbians and Slovenians proclaimed their own state and the next day the Ottoman Empire signed the Armistice of Mudros. At the beginning of November Austria and Bulgaria withdrew from the war and sued for peace terms with Wilson. On 4 November Austria-Hungary made peace with Italy and the Allies on the Western Front advanced to the Meuse. In England the newly-enfranchised female voters were told that politics were in 'a depraved state' but that they should support Lloyd George in the forthcoming elections to get 'a real peace'. Finally the Germans realized that they had lost. On 9 November, Kaiser Wilhelm abdicated and Germany became a Republic. In Austria-Hungary the Emperor Charles I abdicated the following day.

Manchester's reaction to the Armistice was described as being the 'burning joy of the moment'. There had been an all-night vigil at the offices of the *Manchester Guardian*, all the lines cleared for news of the official announcement. At 10.30am flags were unfurled at the offices of the *Guardian* and *Evening News* and at 11.00am people crowded into Albert Square and watched the flag being hoisted above the Town Hall. Then came the historic announcement for which everyone had been waiting, in the immortal words of Lloyd George '... at the eleventh minute of the eleventh hour of the eleventh month ... this morning came to end the cruellest and most terrible War that has ever scourged mankind. I hope we may say that thus,

President Woodrow Wilson visits Manchester in 1918. (*Courtesy of Manchester Central Library Local Studies Collection*)

Market Street, Manchester, *c.*1913.

this fateful morning, came an end to all wars'. Hostilities had ceased and the Great War was over. Factory sirens sounded across the city and everyone flung open their windows like imprisoned birds wanting to escape a long captivity. Initially many folk cried, with both relief and also sadness for those who would never come home. Then tears turned to laughter and by the afternoon jubilation was the main mood. Munitions workers flooded into the streets. Shops, offices and warehouses closed. Manchester Grammar School declared a half-day holiday. The bells of the Town Hall were rung and down in nearby Salford Quays tugs tooted their whistles. Folk trimmed their hats in red, white and blue and as night fell the lighting restrictions were lifted and the whole city lit up. Musicians seemed to strike up everywhere and there was impromptu dancing in the streets. A small donkey cart containing a few working girls, shawls over their heads, cheering and waving flags, made its way along Market Street. Other girls in the street 'danced a few steps of a wild foxtrot'. As the *Manchester Guardian* reported 'the night's celebrations were exuberant, spontaneous and raucous'. The City of Manchester had made a vital contribution to the war effort on the military fronts as well as on the home front. The Manchester Regiment had formed an extra thirty-eight battalions during the course of the war in addition to the pre-existing establishment of two Regular, two Militia and six Territorial battalions, a feat mainly due to the huge number of volunteers from the city. The regiment was awarded seventy-two battle honours and eleven Victoria Crosses during the war but paid a heavy price with the loss of 13,770 men. So it was a celebration tinged with sadness at the memory of so many who had selflessly made the supreme sacrifice in order that others could live in freedom. Nearly 2,500 years ago the Greek historian Thucydides said that history was cyclical, that the same sort of things would go on happening over and over again; and so it proved to be in the case of the Great War, 'the war to end all wars'. Within twenty years the world would once again be at war.

Index